WRITING

INTERMEDIATE

MARIE-CHRISTINE BOUTIN,
SUZANNE BRINAND & FRANÇOISE GRELLET

WRITING

INTERMEDIATE

OXFORD SUPPLEMENTARY SKILLS

SERIES EDITOR: ALAN MALEY

OXFORD UNIVERSITY PRESS

Oxford University Press
Walton Street, Oxford OX2 6DP

Oxford New York Toronto Madrid
Delhi Bombay Calcutta Madras Karachi
Kuala Lumpur Singapore Hong Kong Tokyo
Nairobi Dar es Salaam Cape Town
Melbourne Auckland

and associated companies in
Berlin Ibadan

Oxford and *Oxford English* are trade marks of
Oxford University Press

ISBN 0 19 453405 7

Set by Promenade Graphics Limited, Cheltenham

Printed in Hong Kong.

Illustrations by:

Christyan Jones
David Langdon
David Murray
Punch

The publishers would like to thank the following for their
permission to reproduce photographs:

Robert Harding

Location photography by Rob Judges

While the publishers have made every effort to trace
copyright holders of published material, we have not been
able to clear permission in every case.

CONTENTS

ACKNOWLEDGEMENTS

This book developed from materials originally written within the framework of the Institut National de Recherche Pédagogique in Paris. We are grateful to colleagues there for their advice and criticisms as well as to Suzy Eboli for her help when the original version of this work was produced.

We would also like to thank all the friends and colleagues who tested this material and made valuable remarks and suggestions.

FOREWORD

This series covers the four skill areas of Listening, Speaking, Reading and Writing at four levels — elementary, intermediate, upper-intermediate and advanced. Although we have decided to retain the traditional division of language use into the 'four skills', the skills are not treated in total isolation. In any given book the skill being dealt with serves as the *focus* of attention and is always interwoven with and supported by other skills. This enables teachers to concentrate on skills development without losing touch with the more complex reality of language use.

Our authors have had in common the following principles, that material should be:

- creative — both through author-creativity leading to interesting materials, and through their capacity to provoke creative responses from students;
- interesting — both for their cognitive and affective content, and for the activities required of the learners.
- fluency-focused — bringing in accuracy work only in so far as it is necessary to the completion of an activity;
- task-based — rather than engaging in closed exercise activities, to use tasks with pay-offs for the learners;
- problem-solving focused — so as to engage students in cognitive effort and thus provoke meaningful interaction;
- humanistic — in the sense that the materials speak to and interrelate with the learners as real people and engage them in interaction grounded in their own experience;
- learning-centred — by ensuring that the materials promote learning and help students to develop their own strategies for learning. This is in opposition to the view that a pre-determined content is taught and identically internalized by all students. In our materials we do not expect input to equal intake.

By ensuring continuing consultation between and among authors at different levels, and by piloting the materials, the levels have been established on a pragmatic basis. The fact that the authors, between them, share a wide and varied body of experience has made this possible without losing sight of the need to pitch materials and tasks at an attainable level while still allowing for the spice of challenge.

There are three main ways in which these materials can be used:

- as a supplement to a core course book;
- as self-learning material. Most of the books can be used on an individual basis with a minimum of teacher guidance, though the interactive element is thereby lost.
- as modular course material. A teacher might, for instance, combine intermediate *Listening* and *Speaking* books with upper-intermediate *Reading* and elementary *Writing* with a class which had a good passive knowledge of English but which needed a basic grounding in writing skills.   *(Alan Maley, Madras 1987)*

INTRODUCTION TO THE TEACHER

The purpose of this book is to help your students to write better and more authentic English.

Our first aim is to familiarize them with *different varieties* of written English: not simply letters and postcards, but also messages, diaries, telegrams or notes. Each of these specific forms of writing has its own rules and conventions, its own vocabulary and organization. This is why we deal with each separately, and the book is divided into eight units, seven devoted to one type of writing, and one covering all of them.

We also believe that the easiest way of learning how to write is not to start from a number of instructions and rules but to *read,* paying close attention to the way the text is structured and written. For this reason, each of the units follows the same progression:

- Students *read and study a few examples* of the form of English the unit deals with.
- Through questions and activities, they are led to *understand the rules* that underlie that form of writing: the order in which the different ideas usually appear, the structures or expressions which are commonly used, etc.
- Students then *start writing* and, through a series of graded exercises, come to produce their own texts.

The exercises we suggest in this book are sometimes meant to be done individually, sometimes in pairs or groups. Writing will therefore be the outcome of a period of study, discovery and discussion in which reading and speaking both play important parts.

1 Postcards

I haven't written
(Tick here) because
- BEEN ON THE ROAD
- NO LEAD IN MY PENCIL
- MET AN ITALIAN ACTOR
- YOU HAVEN'T EITHER
- BEEN SICKER THAN A DOG
- RAN OUT OF BLANK CHEQUES
- TOO MANY KIDS
- WOULDN'T YOU LIKE TO KNOW
- FLAT BROKE
- DIARY FULL
- HUSBAND TOO NARROW-MINDED

Other Reasons
_____
_____

1 Familiarization

Postcards are usually associated with holidays, when people do not
feel like writing long letters, and prefer to send a few informal lines to
their friends and family.

Task 1

When do *you* send postcards? Tick the box or boxes. Add any other
occasions you can think of.

- [ ] when you are on holiday
- [ ] as a thank you letter
- [ ] as a business letter
- [ ] on birthdays and other festivals
- [ ] other

Compare your ideas with a partner's — do you both send postcards
on the same occasions?

Task 2

Even though they *are* informal, postcards are usually written according to a number of unwritten 'rules'.

In pairs, look at these four postcards and fill in the table that follows with the appropriate words or expressions.

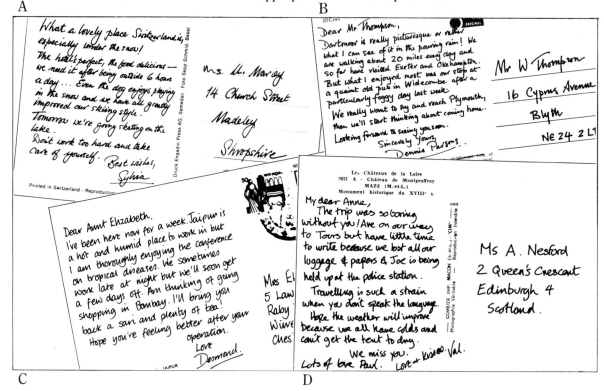

A

What a lovely place Switzerland is, especially under the snow!
The hotel's perfect, the food delicious — we need it after being outside 6 hours a day ... Even the dog enjoys playing in the snow and we have all greatly improved our skiing style.
Tomorrow we're going skating on the lake.
Don't work too hard and take care of yourself. Best wishes,
Sylvia

Ms. M. Marley
14 Church Street
Madeley
Shropshire

B

Dear Mr Thompson,
Dartmoor is really picturesque or rather what I can see of it in the pouring rain! We are walking about 20 miles every day and so far have visited Exeter and Okehampton. But what I enjoyed most was our stop at a quaint old pub in Widecombe after a particularly foggy day last week.
We really want to try and reach Plymouth, then we'll start thinking about coming home.
Looking forward to seeing you soon.
Sincerely yours,
Dennis Parsons.

Mr W Thompson
16 Cyprus Avenue
Blyth
NE 24 2 L1

C

Dear Aunt Elizabeth,
I've been here now for a week. Jaipur is a hot and humid place to work in but I am thoroughly enjoying the conference on tropical diseases. We sometimes work late at night but we'll soon get a few days off. Am thinking of going shopping in Bombay. I'll bring you back a sari and plenty of tea!
Hope you're feeling better after your operation.
Love
Desmond.

Mrs El
5 Law
Raby
Winve
Ches

D

Les Châteaux de la Loire
8051 A - Château de Montgeoffroy
MAZE (M.-et-L.)
Monument historique du XVIII s.

My dear Anne,
The trip was so boring without you! Are on our way to Tours but have little time to write because we lost all our luggage & papers & Joe is being held up at the police station.
Travelling is such a strain when you don't speak the language.
Hope the weather will improve because we all have colds and can't get the tent to dry.
We miss you.
Lots of love Paul.   Love + kisses Val.

Ms A. Nesford
2 Queen's Crescent
Edinburgh 4
Scotland.

	Examples from postcards
Greeting (if any)	
Salutation	*Best wishes,* (A)
Contractions used	*I've been here now for a week* (C)
Words that have been omitted	
Type of words omitted	

Task 3

Now look at the four postcards again. What do they tell you about the relationships between the people who wrote the postcards and the people they wrote to?

Individually, pick out all the words and expressions that helped you to decide. Discuss your answers with a partner. Did you come to the same conclusions?

Postcard	Relationship	Expressions
A		
B		
C		
D		

Task 4

Look at the examples of the different kinds of structures that can be used in writing postcards. Find other examples from the postcards in Task 2.

1 to describe the place where you are:
   How lovely Oxford is under the sun!
   . . . .
   . . . .
   . . . .

2 to describe your present activities:
   We're enjoying our tour through the Greek Islands.
   . . . .
   . . . .

3 to describe your plans:
   We're going to spend a few days with Uncle George next week.
   . . . .
   . . . .

4 to mention the person you're writing to:
   Hope you're feeling better after your operation.
   . . . .
   . . . .

2   Transfer and practice

Task 1

Think about the tenses used in the postcards to refer to past, present or future events.

Match columns **A** and **B** so as to get correct and meaningful sentences. The first one has been done for you.

A	**B**
1 To-morrow	we spent 2 days in Corfu.
2 Next week	we're enjoying the sun & doing nothing.
3 Yesterday	we've had rain every day.
4 Today	we're thinking of taking the boat to Capri.
5 Every day	we drove along the Loire Valley.
6 Last week	we'll probably be back home with you.
7 Lately/recently	it's been extremely cold.
8 So far	we go for a walk.

Which of the descriptions below refer to the sentences you have made? Write your completed sentences next to the appropriate description.

Description	Sentence
a past action or event	
b future action or event	*Tomorrow we're thinking of taking the boat to Capri.*
c present action or event	
d action or event which began in the past and is not yet finished	
e something which is done regularly	

Task 2

In pairs, read carefully through the extract from a holiday brochure. Which of the following sentences could you write at the end of the second day?

	Yes	No	
1	☐	☐	We've had a lovely time so far.
2	☐	☐	We'll go to Nuremberg.
3	☐	☐	The Rhine Valley was spectacular!
4	☐	☐	We did not like the Channel crossing.
5	☐	☐	We made friends with delightful people in the group.
6	☐	☐	We'll soon be in Vienna.
7	☐	☐	We're spending 2 days in Vienna at the end of the week.
8	☐	☐	We both like Nuremberg very much.
9	☐	☐	We've had a delicious meal in Ostend.

Task 3

Now write the postcard you might send to a friend at the end of the
fifth day of your holiday.

The Rhineland, Southern Germany, Vienna and Salzburg

Day 1   London/Dover - Ostend - Eindhoven - Rhineland area.
Leave Victoria Station at 07.30 hrs. (optional) this morning for Dover for the Channel crossing to Ostend, (see page 9). Now board your coach for the drive through Belgian countryside by way of Eindhoven to the Rhineland area for overnight.

Day 2   Rhine cruise - Würzburg - Nuremberg. You'll see some marvellous scenery today, following the Rhine south-west along its most spectacular stretches — the Rhine Gorge and Lorelei Rock with its picturesque castles and riverbank towns, and Rüdesheim, in the heart of the Rhine winelands, then you'll soon be driving along the fast motorway west to Nuremberg in Southern Germany, once its best-preserved medieval city, now better known for its toys and joyful atmosphere.

Day 3   Nuremberg - Regensburg - Linz - Vienna. Now you're in Bavaria. The morning's drive brings you to Regensburg and your first sight of the Danube, then takes you on south of the river to Passau and the Austrian border. Once through Linz, join the fast motorway which will take you to Vienna.

Day 4   Leisurely day in Vienna.
Full programme of optional excursions.

Day 5   Morning Vienna to Salzburg - Afternoon at leisure.
Don't miss the optional sightseeing in Salzburg.

Day 6   Salzburg - Stuttgart - Karlsruhe - Coblenz - The Rhineland. An early start this morning, by-passing Munich then northwards travelling all the time on the fast motorway to Coblenz, then into the Rhineland for your overnight stop.

Day 7   The Rhineland area - Ostend - Dover/London. A comfortable drive this morning to embark at Ostend for the cross-Channel ferry to Dover. Train to London's Victoria Station arriving at 20.30 hrs.

DEPARTURES

Friday: 1 Apr.
Saturday: 30 Apr; 28 May, 27 Aug.
Meals: on half-board basis, bed and breakfast in Vienna.
Accommodation: 4 nights with bath or shower, 2 nights with hot and cold.

3   Consolidation

Task 1

Here are some holiday snapshots. Choose one (or more) from columns 1 and 2, decide who you are going to write to (column 3), and write an appropriate postcard. Try to use some of the vocabulary below.

1

2

3

a girl/boyfriend
your uncle
one of your parents' friends
(whom you don't know very well)
your boss
a colleague or fellow student

The weather	What you see. Where you stay	Your moods and feelings
cold freezing	superb breathtaking spectacular	tired exhausted
rainy windy	magnificent marvellous beautiful	bored
foggy misty	lovely attractive charming	disappointed
gorgeous	picturesque friendly hospitable	fed up
sunny hot	comfortable cosy famous	
warm mild		delighted
	dull boring uninteresting	interested
	unattractive disappointing ugly	excited
	expensive noisy crowded dirty	enthusiastic
	filthy smelly	

your postcard:

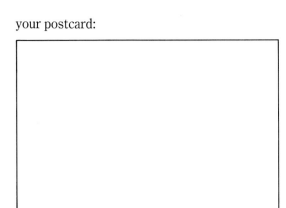

Task 2

Read the following letter and write the postcard Angie would send to one of her friends. Remember those 'rules' for writing postcards.

DEVON
(August).

Dear Mum and Dad,

It's great to be back in Devon after having spent such a long time stuck in London. I've spent this week doing all the things I really enjoy.

On Monday, Matthew and I spent the whole day horse riding on Dartmoor. We rode all the way out to that old barn by the river and then we had a picnic. On the way home, Matthew fell off his pony three times. The last time it happened he fell straight into a stream. He says that he'll never go riding with me again!

We've been to the beach two or three times. The weather isn't too bad, so we were able to go swimming. The only problem at this time of year is that the beaches are so crowded that it's almost impossible to find somewhere to sit.

Last night, a group of us went into Exeter. We had a beautiful meal in a restaurant near the cathedral. We all ate far too much.

As you can see, I'm having a lovely time.

See you soon,

Lots of love
Angie.

Task 3

Buy a postcard and send it to someone who knows English. You could tell them about a holiday or a weekend or an excursion or visit you have been on recently.

2

Diaries

DIARY FOR 1953

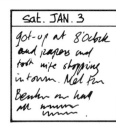

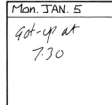

1 Familiarization

There is one important difference between a diary and most other forms of writing — a diary is usually written to be read by the writer only. A postcard, a message or a letter are obviously written to one or more specific people. Diaries, on the contrary, other than those written by some politicians and other famous people, who aim for publication, are not meant to be read by anyone else.

Task 1

In small groups, read through these diary extracts. What sort of people do you think wrote them?

1

Monday   January 25th
NEW MOON
Couldn't do my Maths homework. Phoned the Samaritans. The nice man on the end of the phone told me the answer was nine-eighths. He was dead kind to someone in despair.

Tuesday   January 26th
The stupid Samaritan got the answer wrong! It's only seven-fifths. I only got six out of twenty. Pandora got them all right. In fact she got a hundred per cent.

2

Lentini, Sunday July 25 — Briefing. We have cut the road near Agira, and our bag of prisoners is sixty-five thousand so far. It is hard to get accurate information here even on what is taking place in the next valley; never in the desert did officers feel so isolated.

3

March 14th, Monday

Hideous night. Mosquito in net and v. large brown bugs in bed. Up and dressed at dawn and went for long walk in hills. Met quaint caravan — drums, spears, etc. No news Sarah's trunk.

4

C. today accused of having stolen a football from gym. Teacher called up, asked if I'd seen it in the house. I said no, but would search the house. Did not find it. Have no doubt C. did steal it, maybe passed it on to some boy who doesn't even go to Brunswick School. This evening C. was evasive, angrily says he is being falsely accused.

Task 2

In the same groups, think about the language used in diaries. These questions will help you.
- How could you tell who wrote the diaries in Task 1?
  Do you find the same sort of clues as to a person's occupation in the letters or postcards they write?
- What kind of things do people mention in their diaries— everyday, routine things or special, unusual events?
- Think of what you did yesterday. Was there anything that you would mention in your diary, if you kept one? If so, what?

Task 3

In pairs, look at the diary extracts again. This time, examine the structures used.

1 Find examples of different ways of writing the date . . . .

. . . .

. . . .

2 Find examples of words omitted:
   a first person subjects (*I*/*we*) . . . .

. . . .

. . . .

   b verbs . . . .

. . . .

. . . .

   c others (e.g. prepositions) . . . .

. . . .

. . . .

3 Find examples of abbreviations:
   a for names . . . .

. . . .

. . . .

   b for other words . . . .

. . . .

. . . .

2   Transfer and practice

In a diary we usually write about events *in chronological order* — i.e.
the order in which they happened. To do this we frequently need to
use time prepositions and adverbs.

Task 1

Here are some short extracts from diaries. Complete them with the
appropriate prepositions taken from this list:
for   in   at   during   about   after   since.
In some cases more than one preposition can be chosen.

1   . . . . . . the evening we went to the cinema. Saw *Star Wars*.
2   Phoned Peter . . . . . . 10 p.m.
3   Still feeling ill. Have been at home . . . . . . the last three days.
4   Took Nancy to Hampton Court . . . . . . that, we had supper in an
    Italian restaurant in Richmond.
5   Postal strike going on. Haven't had any mail . . . . . . last
    Wednesday.
6   Had my interview today. It was fine . . . . . . the first 10 minutes,
    then everything started going wrong.
7   Quiet day at the office. No one called . . . . . . the afternoon: a
    record!
8   Michael finally arrived . . . . . . lunchtime.

When you have completed the exercise, compare your answers with
a partner's. If you have different answers, decide whether both are
correct. Where more than one answer is correct, decide how the
meaning of the sentence is changed by the preposition you use. Are
there any other possible answers?

Task 2

In groups, look at the picture opposite and discuss what you think is
happening, and how people feel.

Now work alone and imagine you are one of the people in the picture.
Write an account in your diary of what happened that day. Use some
of the following adverbs:
at first   then   later on   afterwards   soon   finally   at last.

Here are some guidelines:
guests/arrive
have drinks/have lunch
relax/spend a quiet afternoon talking
be hot
have a swim/a pool
an accident/whirlpool sucking in swimmers
shouts/screams/panic
be frightened/hurt/startled/embarrassed

"This always has to happen when we've got company."

3   Consolidation

Task 1

In pairs, read through this extract from an article written after the big
New York blackout of 1977. Ask your partner or your teacher if you
don't understand anything. Discuss what you might have done if you
had been there.

THE BIG NEW YORK BLACKOUT

On a very hot evening last week, a summer storm knocked out high-
voltage power lines in the New York suburbs, and within the hour
returned 9 million people to the dark, heat and disquiet of a pre-electric
age.

For a night and a day, nothing worked except telephones, transistor
radios . . . Subways ran dead. Elevators hung high in their shafts. Water
pumps failed, and with them sinks, tubs and toilets. Streetlights and
spotlights went out.

And in the ghettos, the thieves and burners were soon in the street,
tearing off the protective metal grills, breaking the shop windows, and
lighting fires. More than 2,000 stores were pillaged, and estimates of
property losses ran as high as $1 billion. . . . Civilization had switched
off.

Now complete this diary entry, written the day after the blackout.
Remember you may omit some words, but you will need to insert
some time adverbs and prepositions to show the sequence of events.

Thursday, July 15th — 1977
. . . . . . after a long sleepless night. Something incredible happened
yesterday.
. . . . . . the station . . . . . . a hard day's work. Was just about to board
the train . . . . . . suddenly all the lights went out. . . . . . . a real panic
. . . . . . the first five minutes, people screamed and rushed to the
street thinking it was the end of the world. . . . . . . they started to
calm down and patiently waited for the electricity to come back. But I
. . . . . . realized it was useless to wait there. So . . . . . . the street,
but everything dark there. Didn't know what to do, where to go.
. . . . . . but all hotels full.
. . . . . . on a bench in Central Park — not very comfortable! Could
not even go to sleep!
Managed to get a lift home at . . . . . . 5 a.m. Was dropped 3 miles
away from here. So . . . . . .
Am . . . . . . home . . . . . . absolutely exhausted. . . . . . . a bath and go
to bed.

Task 2

Choose one of the following people and write his or her diary for the
same day:

a student   a shopkeeper
a housewife   an executive

Task 3

This is Edward Mason's diary for May 20th.

MAY 20th

Had a busy day in the garden
today. Interesting chat with
Simon Hendry about his roses.
Then mowed the lawn, but
lawn mower broke down. Wonder
why! In the afternoon, enjoyed
looking at apple tree. Lovely blossom.
Went to bed early.

Write *either* his wife Martha's diary for the same day *or* his neighbour Simon's diary for the same day.

Remember the diary-writing conventions and give details of what really happened. Use the pictures below to help you.

These words may be useful. *fence post   (to) fence ornamental pond   swarm of bees*

Task 4

In pairs, read this extract from a diary. Who or what wrote it?

it is all down to it being it is because it is

you could have fooled me that's not how it felt to me

wave about move about, in the wind

a shoot a young, small plant, just coming out

the stem the long part of a plant, between the roots and the flower

A field, February 20
Well, dear diary, today I and some of the others got born. Premature, as it turns out. They say it is all down to it being a mild winter but you could have fooled me. It is bloody freezing.

February 28
Nothing much happened today except that a kid tiptoed through us. Waiting to flower is very boring. There is nothing for a tulip to do except wave about, and you cannot do a lot of that when you are only a shoot.

To pass the time, some of us had a discussion about what colour we would like to be when we come out. The one next to me on the right-hand side said it would like to be yellow, to go with its green stem. The one on the left-hand side says black, now that's an unusual colour. Speaking for myself, I would like to be red.

March 7
We are all yellow. So much for that bit of excitement!

Now write a diary entry for a plant, animal or other object of your choice.

3 Messages

1 Familiarization

A message is a very practical form of brief written communication. Messages are usually written in a hurry, and either left or sent, often by hand, to someone who is absent at the time but who will probably be arriving soon.

Task 1

When do *you* leave messages?

- [ ] to give someone important information
- [ ] to warn someone of something
- [ ] to tell someone not to do something
- [ ] to give an explanation
- [ ] to apologize for something
- [ ] to tell someone of a change of plans
- [ ] to pass on details of a telephone call
- [ ] other

Compare your answers with a partner's. How many other situations can you think of in which you would write a message?

Task 2

Even though messages are usually written in a hurry, they still follow certain 'rules' of structure.

Work in pairs. The four messages which follow were written on the same day.
In what order were they written?
What do you think happened — why were they written?

A

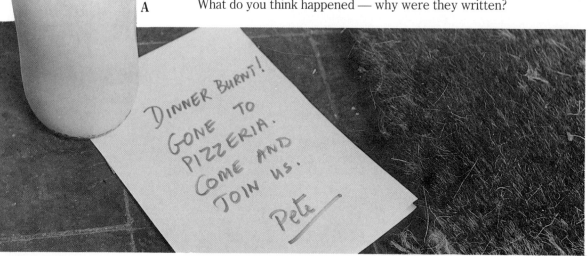

> DINNER BURNT!
> GONE TO
> PIZZERIA.
> COME AND
> JOIN US.
>   Pete

B

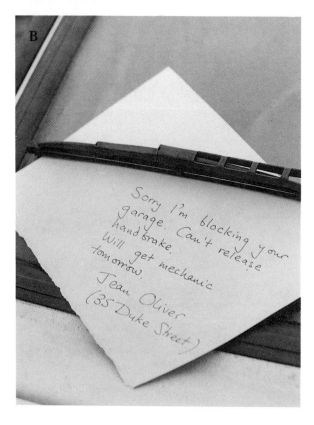

> Sorry I'm blocking your
> garage. Can't release
> hand brake.
> Will get mechanic
> tomorrow.
> Jean Oliver
> (35 Duke Street)

C

> Mr and Mrs Dennis
> will be late — can't
> use their car. Said
> not to wait for them.

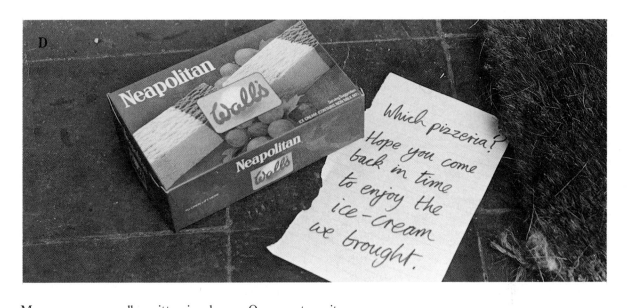

Messages are usually written in a hurry. One way to write more
quickly is to write less — to leave some words out.

Task 3

Study the four messages again and complete the table below. First,
tick each type of word which can be omitted. Then find at least one
example of each type in the messages and write it in the table.

Type of word	Examples
☐ (to) be	**A** *Dinner (is) burnt!*
☐ (to) have	
☐ other verbs	
☐ nouns	
☐ pronouns	
☐ articles	

2 Transfer and practice

Task 1

Messages are often used to apologize, give an explanation or give
instructions. Here are some examples of expressions used in
messages. Think of at least one more for each column. Look back at
the messages in Section 1 for some ideas.

Explaining what happened	*Apologizing*	*Explaining one's plans*	*Wishes*	*Giving instructions*
Gone for 5 minutes.	Forgot to come at 4.	Back at 4.		Don't wait for me.

Task 2

Look at the following cartoon and write the message which Martha
left for Ned.

Task 3

Write appropriate messages for these situations.

1   You're walking along the beach and find a bottle with a message
    inside. What does it say?
2   You're walking past a prison when a tiny piece of paper flutters
    down. It's a message from a prisoner. Write the message.
3   You've just arrived at Heathrow Airport. The friends you
    expected are not there to meet you; but they have left a note.
    What is their message?

Now compare your messages with a partner's. Are they very
different?

3   Consolidation

Task 1

In pairs, think about the messages you have written in the past week
or so. Write them down, and give them to your partner to work out
the circumstances in which you wrote them. Do the same with your
partner's messages.

Task 2

In groups, think of up to four situations in which you might really
need to write messages, and up to four more unlikely situations (like
the bottle with a message in).

Individually, write one or two messages of each kind. Pass them
round the group to compare them.

Task 3

Write a message to your teacher (for example, explaining why you
have to miss a class, or have not done some work), to a friend (for
example, explaining why you can't meet, or where you've gone) and
to your family or landlady (for example, saying what time you'll be in
this evening).

> Dear Santa,
>   I think you made a misstake. I wanted a pinball mashine for Xmas and you sent me a baby sister. I am returning her to you in a seprate packaje in exchange for a pinball mashine.
>
>   Thank you,
>   Kenny Ferndern

1 Familiarization

Informal letters can be written for a variety of reasons, using a variety of words, but they will always have some purpose behind them, and follow some 'rules'. The Guide to letter writing on page 30 shows the structure and layout of a typical informal letter.

Task 1

When do *you* write informal letters?

- ☐ to apply for a job
- ☐ to apologize
- ☐ to send an invitation
- ☐ to thank someone for something
- ☐ to complain
- ☐ to accept or refuse an invitation
- ☐ to order goods by post
- ☐ to send your news to a friend

Compare your answers with a partner's.

Each of the following sections deals with a particular type of informal letter: invitation, acceptance or refusal, thanks, apology.

2 Letters of invitation

These are informal invitations, sent to friends, relatives or acquaintances to invite them to a special occasion.

Task 1

Look at the Guide to letter writing on page 30 and list the expressions Margery uses to invite Sally and Simon.

Here are some other expressions of invitation:

We were wondering if you and Simon could join us
Could you come for . . . on . . .?
What about coming . . .
We'd like you to . . .
We'd like to invite you to . . ./for . . .

If you are very keen for the person to accept, you may try to persuade him or her like this:

We do hope that you'll both be able to come.
(We) do hope you'll join us.
Do try to be there.
I'm really looking forward to seeing you.

Informal letters usually have an opening or *introduction*, which may not be the central theme of the letter. For example, you may thank the person for her letter, or apologize for not having written sooner.

The *body* of the letter is the invitation. You mention:
• the nature of the invitation (e.g. lunch, dinner, a party)
• the date and the time
• the reason, if any (e.g. a birthday, a visit of a mutual friend)
• the people who will be there (this is not essential).

The *ending* of the letter may be only one sentence long. It is usually some kind of persuasive formula.

The *close* as in all informal letters, depends on how well you know the person, and how close you are to them.

Task 2

Now complete the following informal invitation:

Dear Claire,

Thank you so much for your nice long letter. I meant to . . . .

. . . . but somehow I . . . .

. . . .

The thing is we are having . . . . next . . . .

. . . . our tenth wedding anniversary with

. . . . It will be quite informal as Paul

hates dressing up. We . . . . if . . . .

. . . . at 8 p.m.

We . . . .

                    Love,

                      Jane

Task 3

People often send printed invitations, even for an informal invitation. You fill in the blanks with the details of your occasion.

Here is an invitation sent by Jan to a friend. Write the letter of invitation she could have written instead of sending this card.

We're having a Party!

at ___4 Topsham Road___

_____ Exeter _____

on ___Saturday, January 14th___

time _____7.30 p.m._____

Hope you can make it!

Mary just back from India.
will be here and wants to see you.
Jan.

RSVP _____

_____

Telephone ___Exeter 49256___

3 Letters of acceptance or refusal

Task 1

Here are three letters of acceptance or refusal. Read them carefully
and then refer to the Guide to letter writing on page 30 as you will
now be able to fill in some more of the boxes.

Task 2

In pairs, read the letters again, and complete the table.
1

My darling,
Of course the answer will
have to be yes. I'm longing to
see you again. If only you didn't
have to spend so much time
abroad these days. I'll be sorry
to give up my tickets for the
concert, but don't worry I'll make
sure that I'm at Heathrow to
meet you. It's a pity you can't
stay a bit longer so that the
children could see you too.
With all my love,

Liz

Dear Julia,
I was awfully glad to get
your card. I was beginning
to think you had forgotten me.
I'm afraid I won't be able
to make it to your party - it's
just before my finals, and I
must do as well as I can.
But I do hope you'll let me
come and see you once the
exams are safely out of the
way.
Wishing you the happiest
of birthdays,

John

Dear Langley,
Of course I remember you well,
and will only be too delighted
for you to come and stay for
a couple of nights. I always
enjoy meeting up with my
former students.
Unfortunately, my wife has
been unwell recently, but she
is now recovering, I am glad
to say. However, we have our
evening meal early, so if you'd
like to join us for supper, please
be here by six-fifteen. I think
the train arrives at about
five to.
Yours sincerely,
James Weatherall

	1	2	3
What is the relationship between the letter writer and the addressee? (Do they know each other well? Are they friends, relatives or what?)			
Is it a letter of refusal or acceptance?			
What is being accepted or refused?			
List the expressions used to accept or refuse.			

Task 3

Read the phrases below. Put a tick next to those that you could use to express acceptance. Put a cross next to those that you could use to express refusal. (Some of the expressions could be interpreted either way.)

☐ I | should | be delighted to . . .
    | would |

☐ I would love to come, but . . .

☐ Of course, we'll . . .

☐ We'll come with pleasure . . .

☐ It would have been lovely to join you, but . . .

☐ It was nice of you to suggest it, but . . .

☐ Thank you so much for your invitation. We're looking forward to seeing you . . .

☐ I wish I could accept your kind invitation . . .

☐ I'm afraid we won't be able to join you all . . .

☐ What a surprise to get your invitation . . .

☐ Yes, we'll be there . . .

☐ Unfortunately we will not be able to . . .

☐ It's such a long time since we last met, so . . .

Compare your answers with a partner's.

Task 4

You have just received the letter below. Consult your diary for the same weekend and reply to your friend's invitation. None of your engagements can be changed, except your Sunday morning tennis, and it takes about one hour to get to your friend's house (and an hour to return, of course).

Monday Nov. 18th

Dear Alison,

Just a few lines to tell you that Mark will be here next weekend. He called last night to tell us the good news. You **must** come and see him. He mentioned you and said how very much he hoped he wasn't going to miss you this time.

Come and have a meal with us — any time.

Looking forward to seeing you.

Love

Frances

P.S. I tried to ring you this morning but my phone's out of order.

SATURDAY

John's birthday.
→ take him to the seaside. (boat?)

SUNDAY

9am Tennis with Mary.

1pm Lunch with the O'Connors.

(Bring holiday slides for projection in the evening.)

4 Letters of thanks

Task 1

Here are several 'thank you' letters written by the same person after Christmas. In pairs, match the letters and the pictures below.

a

b

c

d

1

Dear Uncle Arthur,

Thank you for your extremely generous Christmas present. I don't know how you guessed, but socks were exactly what I wanted.

What socks, too! I have looked it up and see that it is the Macpherson tartan. And how clever of you to remember that I take size seven!

2

Dear Aunt Millie,

How very kind of you to remember me at Christmas! And with socks, too! In fact socks were quite the nicest present I received — size ten was just right, and the very delicate mauve will go excellently with a yellow suit. I must try to get one.

3

Dear Mrs Thimble,

I can't tell you how touched I am that you still go on remembering us 'children' (as I suppose you still think of us!!) every year. And socks were just what I needed. I particularly like the pretty blue ribbons they do up with — they match perfectly the bluebells on the matinee jacket you gave me last Christmas. I shall certainly think of you every time I wear them.

4

Dear Great-uncle Alexander,

I scarcely know what to say! I must admit I had been secretly hoping that someone would give me socks — and you did! Socks are always handy to have — and yours were so cleverly and appropriately Christmassy. I don't think I have ever seen socks with a pattern of holly and mistletoe before, though my favourites are the 'Yuletide Lafter' pair. Some of the jokes printed on them are almost too good to keep hidden under one's trouser-leg!

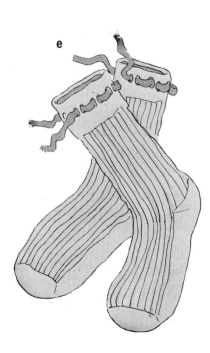

5

Dear Great-aunt Tilly,

I must write at once to thank you for your magnificent present. I can't tell you what my feelings were when I opened that huge parcel and found it contained — a pair of socks!

It was very clever of you to choose a pair with one red and one grey. They make a great change from the ordinary run of socks, and I shall keep them for very special occasions. And how thoughtful of you to remember that my right foot is two inches longer than my left!

I hope you haven't been having any more trouble with your eyesight recently.   *A Book of Fub* Michael Frayn

Task 2

Underline all the expressions used by the person to thank the people he writes to.

Task 3

Write a polite letter of thanks for something you did not want to receive.

Task 4

You were invited to the party below and, in spite of the way the evening ended, you feel you ought to write to the hostess and thank her.

Write the letter. Remember you should:

- thank the person
- say a few words about the party (why it was pleasant, interesting, friendly, etc.)
- add one or two sentences as a conclusion.

'It was one of those games supposed to start the party off with a swing.'

5   Letters of apology

As with any letters, the tone of a letter of apology varies according to who you are writing to, and what you are apologizing for.

Task 1

Here are some examples of people, and reasons for apologizing. Tick any to whom or about which you might write a letter of apology. Compare your answers with a partner's.

- ☐ aunt
- ☐ parent
- ☐ girlfriend/boyfriend
- ☐ husband/wife
- ☐ forgetting a birthday
- ☐ breaking a glass
- ☐ losing a book
- ☐ spilling something
- ☐ treading on the cat
- ☐ boss
- ☐ colleague
- ☐ teacher
- ☐ neighbour
- ☐ not completing work
- ☐ failing an exam
- ☐ crashing a car

Task 2

Here are two letters, both written by the same man, but to two different people. He is friendlier with one of them. The two letters have been mixed up. Read the sentences carefully and re-write them as two separate letters. Pay particular attention to the level of informality of the language.

Compare your versions of the two letters with a partner's.

Finally, still working with your partner, underline the expressions of apology used.

- Dear Peter,
- Dear Mr Miller,
- I'm sorry about last night.
- I am awfully sorry for what happened yesterday.
- I'm afraid I must have spoiled your party and I feel really bad about it all.
- I didn't mean to spoil your party, but your boss was very irritating.

- Please excuse me for what I said. You know how worked up I get when people talk politics; I lose all my self-control.
- I do apologize for my disgraceful behaviour. I should never have started talking about politics.
- When your boss mentioned this new political scandal, I knew I would lose my temper; I should have kept off the subject.
- So when he started going on about this new political scandal, I just couldn't keep my mouth shut. I should have kept out of it all.
- Sorry, Peter!
- Do excuse me, please!
- I hope this will not affect your promotion in any way.
- I just hope you will get your promotion all right.
- It was all my fault, I was your guest; next time I'll behave myself, I promise!
- I know the party was very important to you and it was inexcusable of me to behave as I did.
- Best wishes,
- Yours,
- Paul
- Paul Mason

Task 3

In the following list of phrases, tick those which express apology.

1 ☐ I'm very/terribly/extremely sorry
2 ☐ I'd like to apologize for . . .
3 ☐ I am sorry to hear about . . .
4 ☐ you couldn't help it
5 ☐ please forgive me for . . .
6 ☐ I really must apologize for . . .
7 ☐ it wasn't your fault
8 ☐ forget it
9 ☐ there was nothing you could have done
10 ☐ sorry to have done this/for doing this
11 ☐ I don't want you to feel bad about it
12 ☐ you must forgive me for
13 ☐ don't worry about it
14 ☐ please accept my apologies for . . .
15 ☐ how stupid of me!
16 ☐ what a shame!
17 ☐ you('ll) have to excuse me

In groups, decide what the other phrases can be used for. Each person in the group takes two of the phrases and briefly notes down a situation in which they could be used. Tell each other your situations. Does everyone agree with them?

Task 4

Write the letter of apology this man sent the next day.

Task 5

In groups, each of you writes an informal invitation, and gives it to another member of the group. Make sure no-one receives more than one invitation.

Each member of the group now writes a letter of acceptance or refusal.

Those who accepted should then write a letter of thanks (or apology!) after the event. Those who refused should imagine they were given a present on the occasion of their own invitation, and write and thank the person who gave them the present.

A guide to letter writing

1

Your address (though this is not necessary if you know the person very well.)
If you omit the full address, you may put your town or village by the date. Do not put both full and part address. You need not include the postcode, though it is advisable.

2

The date
e.g. Saturday, March 1st, 1985
    Tuesday, June 14th, 1985
or   (more informal)
    9 (th) Sept (ember) 1985
    9.9.1985
    The year is often omitted.

3

Beginning the letter
Here are some of the expressions you can use as salutations. Find some more in the letters in this unit.
Dear Sally,
Dear Mr Brown,

. . . .
. . . .

---

1 ⌐ The Elms,
    2 Victoria Terrace,
    Oxford
    OX2 ODG
2 ☐ January 18 th

3 ☐ Dear Sally,
4 ☐ Thank you for your lovely birthday card I haven't written sooner as I
5 ☐ wanted to invite you round and could never find a suitable time .
    We're having a small party next Friday night to celebrate Tom's return from Canada, and we would be very happy if you and Simon could join us here, around 8.p.m.
    Do come if you can . It will be quite informal.

6 ☐ Looking forward to seeing you.

    7 ☐ Yours,
        Margery.

4

A possible and common beginning: you thank the person you are writing to for his/her letter . . .
Here are two ways of doing so. Find others in this unit.
Thanks for . . .
Many thanks for . . .

. . . .
. . . .

and you apologize for not having written before:
Find other expressions in the letters in this unit.
I must apologize for not writing . . .
I really should have written sooner . . .

. . . .
. . . .

5

In most letters, you will use one or more of the following functions.
Look at the letters in this unit and find at least one phrase expressing:
apology . . . .

. . . .
thanks . . . .

. . . .
an invitation . . . .

. . . .
acceptance . . . .

. . . .
refusal . . . .

. . . .

6

A common ending: you mention future correspondence, visits, etc.
Find further endings in this unit.
I'll write again soon.
We're longing to hear from you.

. . . .
. . . .

7

The close
Find three more expressions which you can use to close a letter. Classify them according to their degree of informality. Number the boxes 1–7, with 1 the most and 7 the least informal.

☐ *Yours,*
☐ *Yours truly,*
☐ *Best wishes,/All the best,*
☐ *Lots of love,/Much love,*
☐ . . . .
☐ . . . .
☐ . . . .

1 Familiarization

The kind of written English used in telegrams is disappearing, expecially in the UK, where telegrams no longer exist as a service. Instead people tend to use the following:

- ☐ the telephone
- ☐ telexes (most firms and businesses are now able to send their own telexes)
- ☐ telephoned messages, which are delivered on the same day anywhere in the UK
- ☐ Intelpost messages, which you write on special forms and which can be delivered on the same day

Task 1

Tick any of the above that you have used. In what circumstances would they be most suitable?

The form of English used for these, when written, is similar to that of the letter, though it is often somewhat abbreviated.

Although telegrams are not sent in Britain any more, they may be sent *to* Britain, as they are still used in many other countries, including the United States.

Task 2

The telegrams which follow form two sets of correspondence by telegram between two people. The two sets have been jumbled. In pairs, sort out the two sets, and arrange the telegrams in order.

Telegrams

Saturday   November 28th
A telegram! Addressed to me! The BBC? No, from my mother:
   ADRIAN STOP COMING
        HOME STOP
   What does she mean 'Stop coming home'? How can I 'stop coming home'? I live here.

a | TAKE DOG TO HOUSE STOP BACK IN THREE DAYS ROSS

b | POSTAL ORDER TO FRANCE IMPOSSIBLE STOP ASK JANE LOVE DEREK

c | TURNER 4 TOWNSEND STREET LONDON LOVE DEREK

d | YOUR DOG UNBEARABLE STOP COME AND GET IT URGENT CHARLES

e | RETURN DELAYED TIL SUNDAY STOP CHANGE MY LONDON EXETER TICKET IN ENGLAND LOVE HELENA

f | CONTACT SOLICITOR EP JONES STOP BACK TOMORROW ROSS

g | DOG WITH RSPCA STOP COURT ACTION BY NEIGHBOURS DISTURBED BY BARKING CHARLES

h | NO MONEY LEFT SEND £50 LOVE HELENA

i | SEND JANE'S ADDRESS LOVE HELENA

j | IMPOSSIBLE HERE STOP BUY ANOTHER IN LONDON DEREK

Set 1 . . . .
Set 2 . . . .

Task 3

In your pairs, one of you takes Set 1 and the other Set 2. Write
nothing down, but each tell your partner the story of what happened
in your set.

Task 4

Now, still working in pairs, each of you take the story your partner
told. Rewrite each message as it would appear in a short letter rather
than in a telegram.

e.g. CONTACT SOLICITOR EP JONES STOP
        BACK TOMORROW

= Can you contact my solicitor, E.P. Jones? I will be back tomorrow.

Set 1

. . . .

. . . .

. . . .

Set 2

. . . .

. . . .

. . . .

. . . .

Next, note down the words which are omitted from the telegram.
What else do you notice about the style of writing in telegrams?

2 Practice and consolidation

The main reason for telegrams being so abbreviated is cost. There is
usually either a basic charge for, e.g. the first 12 or 20 words, and
then a charge per word for anything more, or, sometimes, a straight
charge per word. This includes the address.

Task 1

You are going to a conference in San Francisco when your briefcase
is stolen. Unfortunately it contained not only your wallet with your
papers, credit cards and cheque book, but also your address book
and diary, and a copy of the talk you have to give at the conference.

You have dealt with the loss of your credit cards and cheque book at the local branch of your bank, but you need to get the diary information, your other address book, a replacement driving licence and the spare copy of your talk.

Telegram your family at once (you cannot get in touch with them on the telephone) to tell them:

- to send you $200 (while you wait for new credit cards from the bank)
- to send you your other address book so that you can visit friends on the way home from the conference
- to contact the local police for a duplicate driving licence
- to get your secretary to send the spare copy of your talk, after making one copy to hold in case of any further emergencies
- your address in San Francisco: Ramada Renaissance Hotel, San Francisco, California

Your family's address is: 10 Roosevelt Avenue, Hertford, Maryland, MD 893241.

All you can spend on the telegram is $20. Each word (including those of the address) costs 50¢ (= $\frac{1}{2}$ dollar). Now write the telegram.

Telegram

western union

MSG. NO.	NO. WDS. CL. OF SVC.	PD.—COLL.	CASH NO.	ACCOUNTING INFORMATION	DATE	FILING TIME	SENT TIME
						A.M. / P.M.	A.M. / P.M.

SEND THE FOLLOWING MESSAGE, SUBJECT TO THE TERMS ON BACK HEREOF, WHICH ARE HEREBY AGREED TO.

☐ OVERNIGHT TELEGRAM
UNLESS BOX ABOVE IS CHECKED THIS MESSAGE WILL BE SENT AS A TELEGRAM.

TO _____ CARE OF OR APARTMENT NO. _____

ADDRESS & TELEPHONE NO. _____

CITY — STATE & ZIP CODE _____

SENDER'S TEL. NO. _____ NAME & ADDRESS _____

OFFICE USE ONLY

EOM (_____ / _____ / _____ / _____ / (CHG. METH.))
(BILL TO)   (ADDRESS)   (CITY - STATE - ZIP)

_____ / _____ / _____ / _____ / _____ / _____ / _____ / _____ / _____ . X-OFF
(CHG.#) (OPR.#) (HF) (PC CODE) (PC AMT.) (GIFT AMT.) (TAX) (AGT. I.D.) (SG)

Task 2

Sonia wants to contact her mother quickly. Her mother has no telephone, so Sonia sent her an Intelpost message.

Now write the telegram Sonia might have written instead of the Intelpost message. Remember, the cost of sending a telegram is 25p per word, including the address. Sonia doesn't want to spend more than £10 on the telegram.

Intelpost	**For Post Office use only**		
A Royal Mail Special Service Transaction number	Time	Year Month Day	
Transmitting office stamp	Receiving office stamp		

To be completed by the sender

Sender's name: *Sonia Whiting*

Address: *℅ Walter Scott Inn, Inverness.*

Postcode:

Phone number: *Inverness 3478*

To be delivered to (name): *Mrs James*

Address: *30, Dane Street, Southampton*

Postcode: *SO9 4YQ*

Phone number: —

Please write your message in the space below in black ink

Service requirement (see notes overleaf for details)
1 ☒ Same day delivery
2 ☐ Next day delivery
3 ☐ Greetings card number

Dear Mum,

Don't get worried when you read this letter. I'm sending it by special delivery because we need money quickly. We've had a small accident, nothing very serious fortunately, but Jeremy's broken his arm and the car is just a wreck. Still, we were lucky that it wasn't worse... Right now, we're staying in Inverness, at the Walter Scott Inn (tel. Inverness 3478) We have to stay here a few days: Jeremy will leave the hospital tonight, but we'd better all rest a few days before travelling back. And we have to do something about the car. Could you please send us £300 here as quickly as you can?

I phoned the insurance, but could you give them a ring and make sure everything is all right. (All the details are in the drawer of my desk.) And if you could ring Jane and cancel our Tuesday appointment?

I'm sorry to send you such a letter but you really mustn't worry. We are all fine now and looking forward to seeing you very soon. Ring us here if you can.

Lots of love,

Sonia.

Task 3

Work in pairs. Each of you imagines a situation in which you need to send a telegram. Write the telegram and give it to your partner. Each of you then writes your partner's telegram out as a letter, to show that you have understood the situation.

1 Familiarization

Formal letters are usually written for business or official purposes.
They usually deal with one theme, with no 'chat' to pad them out.
They are usually written to people you do not know well.

6

Formal letters

Task 1

Tick the boxes to show when you would write formal letters.

☐ to a relative you don't know well
☐ to a friend you have quarrelled with
☐ to apply for a job
☐ to complain about faulty goods
☐ to complain to a neighbour about noise
☐ to your bank manager

Compare your answers with a partner's.

In this unit, we shall deal with only two of the most common types:
letters of application for a job, and letters of complaint.

2 Letters of application

Task 1

In pairs, read this letter. Do you think the writer will get the job?
Why?

To Messrs. Plugg and Gaskett, Ltd., Motor Engineers
Dear Mr Plugg and Gaskett, — I see by your advert that you require a
junior Clerk that is quick at figures. You say you woold prefer one just
left School, well I have just left School so pheraps I woold do? I was 3rd
in my class for Maths and Top for Algebra, but pheraps you woold not
re-quire any Algebra? I was farely good at most subgects exept English
grammer and competition, so pheraps you will let me know? I am very
intrested in Motor Enginering and I am sure you woold find me just right
for the job.

Yours truly,

J. Hoop

What kind of letters do employers like to receive? Tick the boxes.

☐ correctly spelled   ☐ detailing your failures
☐ containing your life history   ☐ detailing relevant experience
☐ friendly   ☐ long and chatty
☐ detailing your qualifications   ☐ short and to the point

Now note down what you think is right and what is wrong with
J. Hoop's letter.

Letter of application

Here is an example of a letter of application. Notice how it is laid out.

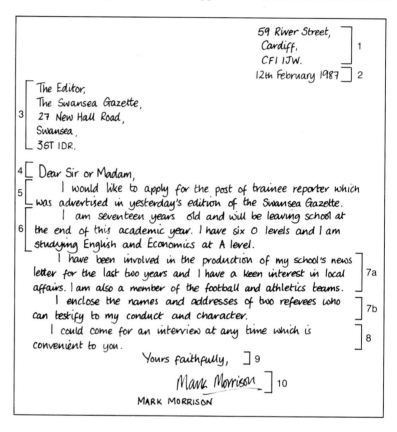

1   Your address. Include your postcode.

2   One blank line in between.
     The date — this is the preferred order, but the month may
     come first. It is better *not* to put the month as a number, e.g.
     12.2.88 — as this can be confusing. American usage would be
     2.12.88.

3   The name and address of the person to whom you are writing.
     Include the postcode.

4   One blank line.
     Salutation (most forms of salutation start with *Dear* . . .,)
     Other possibilities are:
     Dear Sirs, (you know there are several people)
     Gentlemen! (several men — US usage)
     Who are you writing to when you start with:
     Dear Madam, ...
     Dear Sir, ...

5   Introduction.
With reference to your advertisement in ... for ...
I am writing in reply to your advertisement ...
I am applying for the position of ... as advertised in ...
I wish to apply for the post of ...

6   Explain why you are applying.
Here the applicant is informing the editor how his qualifications
match those required. He could have used some kind of formula
to introduce his explanation, such as:
I feel that my qualifications match your requirements ...
My qualifications are as follows ...
I feel I would be suitable for this post because ...
I wish to gain experience of ...
Having already worked as ... for (time) I wish to extend my
experience/feel I could be useful to you ...

7a Give further details.
The details given here may have been asked for in the
advertisement. An employer may want to know if a school-
leaver has held any positions of responsibility. Or the applicant
may feel they are of interest to the employer. But you should
not spend too much time on such details.

7b *Please find enclosed/I enclose ...*
... the names and addresses of ... referees
... my curriculum vitae/CV (personal data sheet — US usage)

8   Make some reference to hearing from the employer.
I { *could come for an interview at any time which would suit you*
       am available for interview ...
       should be glad to attend an interview ...
I look forward to hearing from you ...

9   The close.
This is usually *Yours faithfully,* where the salutation is *Dear Sir,*
etc.
Yours sincerely, is used with a salutation such as
Dear Mr Brown,/Dear Mrs Jones,
Yours respectfully,/truly, should be avoided in modern British
usage

10 The signature.
Sign in your usual 'formal' way — e.g. as on your identity card
or on cheques. It is advisable to print your name afterwards as
people's signatures are often illegible.

Note that a letter of application should always look neat. Well-typed
letters look good, but some employers specify handwritten letters.

Task 2

Choose one of these advertisements for a job and write your letter of application.

YOUTH TRAINING SCHEME

Looking for a good start?

The Post Office — one of the UK's largest employers and a major participant in the Government Youth Training Scheme — has a number of local vacancies for young people wishing to gain valuable work experience and training in the following area of its business:

SUB-POST OFFICE AND RETAIL

No formal academic qualifications are required

The Post Office is an equal oppportunity employer and applications are welcome from all 16 year old school leavers regardless of sex, ethnic background or religion. Disabled applicants up to the age of 21 will also be considered. For further details please contact:

Mr B S Ahluwalia, Youth Training Officer, Paddington District Office, London W2 1AA. Telephone: 239 2889

THE POST OFFICE

DESIGNERS GUILD

We are market leaders in the Design, manufacture and distribution of high quality furnishing fabrics, wall papers, and accessories.

We are currently seeking

TWO ASSISTANT CREDIT CONTROLLERS

to join our young credit control team who form part of our busy Accounts Department in our offices, situated close to White City tube.

The successful applicant will be responsible for running a section of the computerised sales ledger, lots of customer contact pleasant telephone manner and at least 1/2 years relevant experience essential.

SALARY IN THE RANGE £6,500-£8,000, HOURS 9 am-5 pm, 4 WEEKS HOLIDAY, INCENTIVE SCHEME, STAFF PURCHASE SCHEME, SEASON TICKET LOAN ETC.

Please write to Miss R Clucas, Designers Guild, 6 Relay Road, London W12 7SJ or tel: 01-743 6322 ext 145 for an application form.

INSPECTOR

Company producing precision plastic mouldings require an experienced inspector for night shift work.

Hours 10pm - 8am, Monday to Friday.
Good rate of pay, 5 weeks annual holiday, and pension scheme.

APPLY:- CHIEF INSPECTOR
PLASRO PLASTICS LTD.,
38 WATES WAY,
MITCHAM. SURREY.

Tel. 01-640 0145

The South London Guardian is looking for an

EXPERIENCED PRESS PHOTOGRAPHER

to join our fast expanding group of free newspapers

Please apply in writing only to

Bruno Turner, Chief Photographer Guardian House, Sandiford Road. Sutton. Surrey SM3 9RN

SOUTH LONDON *Guardian*

Greengrocery Assistant

Ealing

Safeway are the world's largest food retailing group. We pride ourselves on providing first-class shopping facilities, the very best in customer service and excellent opportunities for the people who work with us.

We now have an opportunity at our store in Ealing for a Greengrocery Assistant.

You should be 18 yrs+ and have a sound greengrocery knowledge, preferably gained within a retail environment.

In return, you will receive an excellent salary of £114-£123 pw after successful completion of trial period, and benefits including a 39 hour week, subsidised staff restaurant and a generous pension scheme.

To apply please contact Brenda Lester, Instore Trainer, Safeway Food Stores Ltd., 20 Town Square, Ealing Broadway Centre, Ealing, London W5.

Tel: 01-840 3502.

(S) SAFEWAY

REDLAND ROOF TILES LTD

require the following staff for their distribution depot in Acton:

CHARGEHAND

A chargehand is required to lead a small team of men within our yard. The successful applicant must be able to demonstrate the leadership qualities and the motivation necessary to get the job done, and must also be thoroughly capable of operating various types of fork-lift trucks. Working a double day shift system, the position is hourly paid with gross wages in the region of £250 per week including bonus, shift rate and a certain amount of overtime.

HGV DRIVER

A driver with Class I or II licence is required to strengthen our fleet operations. Previous experience in operating mechanically off-loaded equipment would be an advantage, although this is not essential as full training will be given to the successful applicant. Rate of pay is £3.00 per hour, with guaranteed 49 hour week in operation, plus weekly productivity bonus.

Excellent holiday entitlement, and first class pension scheme will apply to both appointments.

Please apply in the first instance to: Mr B T McKay, Redland Roof Tiles Ltd. British Railway Sidings, Horn Lane, Acton W3 Telephone 01-993 7701

Task 3

Here is the curriculum vitae (CV) of a woman who intends to send a
letter of application in reply to this advertisement of 19 January.
Write the letter.

EXPERIENCED PERSON REQUIRED, nursery nurse training an advantage, to look after 7-month-old baby, immediate start. Live-in, generous free time, but flexibility essential. Non-smoker. Write: Johnson-Price, 9 Ormsby Close, Great Missenden, Bucks.

```
Name:   Mason Elizabeth Mary

Date of birth:  16th June 1962

Present address:  c/o Bramwell
                  6 Cyprus Drive
                  Maidenhead
                  BERKS
                  SL6 5D2

Permanent address:   6 Milldale Road
                     King's Lynn
                     NORFOLK
                     PC30 45W

Previous jobs:  Sept. 1985 - present

                Nanny to baby and toddler

                April 1983 - September 1985

                Mother's help to family with three small

                children including new-born baby.

                Sept. 1982 - April 1983

                Au-pair in France

                Sept. 1980-June 1982

                Secretarial college (gained Diploma)

Other qualifications:

                Driving licence, good knowledge of French

                and some German.  Experience of cooking/catering.

Reason for wishing to change job:

                Current employers moving to Hong Kong
```

Task 4

Read the following letter of application and replace the underlined sentences with more appropriate ones from pages 36–37.

---

4 New Street,

Birmingham,

B3 3EL

13th February 1987

Brown and Mason Ltd,

4 Broad Street,

Leeds

LS14 1ND

Dear Mr Brown and Mr Mason,

I fell upon your advertisement for the post of personal secretary in yesterday's Pullman's Gazette and would like to be examined for the post.

I am 22, and since I left school six years ago I have worked in three different places, first as a junior clerk on general office duties and then as a shorthand typist for three years. For the last year, I have been taking an intensive secretarial training course in commercial practice. I feel that I just correspond to the type of person you are looking for. You will find in this letter a full list of details about my education and experience.

I shall be glad to send you the name of two people who know me well and who could give out their own impressions about my work. I should be glad to come and see you whenever you feel like it.

Yours sincerely,

Eva Marshall

Eva Marshall

3   Letters of complaint

If you wish to defend your rights as a consumer or make yourself heard when you are dissatisfied about something, it is often necessary to write a letter of complaint. It can sometimes be sent to a newspaper, but you will usually send it to the person responsible for your problem (e.g. the owner of the restaurant if you complain about a meal, the manufacturer of something you bought, etc.).

Task 1

Have you ever written a letter of complaint? When might you write a formal letter of complaint?

☐ when you have been sold poor quality goods

☐ when a train was late

☐ when you had something stolen

☐ when you didn't receive something you had ordered by post and paid for

☐ when your neighbours made a lot of noise

☐ when you had a bad meal in a restaurant

Task 2

You saw the advertisement below in a newspaper and decided to buy this wonderful lighter:

⟨**NEW!**⟩   *THE PERFECT LIGHTER*

★**Economical:** uses no gas or batteries

★**Quick:** lights your cigarette twice as fast as an ordinary lighter

★**Special Offer:** only **£2**

post to: **LIGHTFAST**, Chesford, Sheffield S9 4EX

Name:...

Address ....

....

....

Send £2 (stamps or postal order)

Four days later, you received this in the post:

In pairs, complete the letter of complaint that you would send to the firm.

```
                                              12 Brooks Lane,
                                              Guildford,
                                              Surrey,
                                              GU4 7QB,
                                              12 December 1987

The Sales Director,
LIGHTFAST,
Chesford,
Sheffield,
S9 4EX,

Dear Sir or Madam,
I saw your advertisement for ...............................
in the Sunday Times last week and immediately sent ..............
.......... in order to ....................................
Imagine my surprise when all I got in return was .................
...................! I could understand a mistake, I might
even pardon a joke, but in this case, your advertisement is a
deliberate lie since a friend of mine who also sent the coupon
got the same result.

I think it's a shame to promise an economical lighter when in
fact ....................................................
Instead of saying it works quickly, you should ...............
........................ And what about 'only' £2:............
..............................

I regard your advertisement as a serious deception and demand
that you send me ............................... immediately.
Otherwise I will take active steps to make sure the Consumers'
Association hears about it.
                    Yours faithfully,

                    Peter Hirsham.

                    Peter Hirsham
```

Task 3

In what order are the following points mentioned in the letter? (Write 1, 2, 3 in the appropriate boxes.)

☐ asking that something be done

☐ complaining, expressing one's dissatisfaction

☐ explaining the situation

Underline the expressions used in the letter in order to complain.

Here are some other expressions you could have used:

- *I'm not going to* | *accept* | *this.*
                put up with
                let this go.
- *I should like to know what* | *you intend* | *to do about it.*
                                  you're going
- *Your attitude is* | *deceitful.*
                   negligent.
- *I don't see why you* . . .
- *It's high time you did something* . . .

Task 4

Here is a form that can be found at Heathrow Airport (London) for travellers to note down what they think about the airport facilities and services.

Write the letter Mr Parsons would have sent if, instead of expressing his dissatisfaction on the card, in the form of notes, he had decided to write a letter to the manager of the airport.

Comments

Heathrow

Name	PARSONS Michael	Date	6 / 7 / 85
Address	6 Barton Road,	Time	12 pm
	Plymouth, PL21 4BT	Flight No if appropriate	

We welcome your comments on services provided at Heathrow. Please place your card in this box.

Had to wait two hours to get my suitcase.

Shops closed at 11pm — no coffee left in machines.

No trolleys available.

We will give our attention to all comments – either dealing with items ourselves or referring them to the organisation responsible.

BAA/F/3687   T2

Task 5

Here are some of the other possible components of a letter of
complaint. In pairs, tick those that you think are essential or useful to
include. In the second box, note the order of appearance (1,2,3 etc.)
of the items. If you think two items are interchangeable, give them
the same number.

a ☐ ☐   the date of the occurrence or purchase
b ☐ ☐   how much you paid
c ☐ ☐   the time of the occurrence or purchase
d ☐ ☐   your feelings on the subject
e ☐ ☐   a threat to report the person responsible
f ☐ ☐   a demand for compensation
g ☐ ☐   a recommendation as to what should have been done
         instead
h ☐ ☐   details of inconvenience to yourself
i ☐ ☐   where | you bought the items
               | the event took place
j ☐ ☐   personal information about yourself
k ☐ ☐   insults

Task 6

Write one or more letters of complaint which would be appropriate to
the situations below.

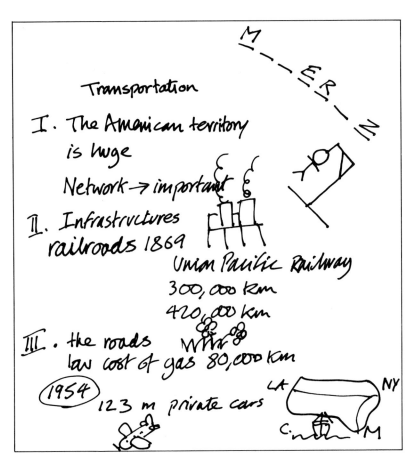

1 Familiarization

Task 1

In groups, discuss, and then write down, when *you* make notes.
Tick any of the following reasons if you have them on your list.

- [ ] to help you remember what you have read
- [ ] to keep track of any ideas that come to you
- [ ] to help you plan an essay
- [ ] to help you plan a letter
- [ ] to help you plan a telephone call
- [ ] to show clearly what the important points of a text or lecture are
- [ ] to help you remember what you have heard (e.g. a lecture)
- [ ] to remind you of the main points of a speech you have to make

Whatever the exact reasons for which *you* use notes, they are obviously to help you remember the main points of something. Therefore, they should be clear, well-structured, not too detailed, and easy to understand even some time after you have made them.

Task 2

Read these notes which a student made on a passage about Queen
Victoria. You will need to study them carefully. In pairs, try to
expand them into a coherent passage about Queen Victoria.

Queen Victoria (1837 – 1901)

— George IV → only child: Charlotte (+ 1817) → William IV
(his brother).
Victoria = his niece.

— very young when she came to the throne ⎤ much loved by
beautiful   ⎦ her people

— Prime Ministers - 1st One (she liked him very much) = Lord
                     Melbourne (refused the Conservative leader
                     Peel)
                  — Peel

— Benjamin Disraeli and William Gladstone
      (alternative Conservative - Liberal governments)

— Married Prince Albert of Saxe -Coburg -Gotha = very
                                       serious -minded.

Consider these questions:

a   What is 1837 — Queen Victoria's date of birth or that of her
    accession to the throne?
b   What does this abbreviation mean: →
c   Whose niece was Queen Victoria?
d   Who refused Peel what?
e   Was Disraeli a Liberal or a Conservative?
f   What did Disraeli and Gladstone do?

In fact several of the answers aren't there, as the notes are rather
ambiguous and so misleading. The next section will explain how to
write more efficient notes.

2 Transfer and practice

Task 1

Now work in pairs or groups of four. Each of you should read through the following passage from John F Kennedy's *A Nation of Immigrants*. Then read it again and check it against one or two of the sets of notes on page 48 to see how well they convey the main points of the passage. Put a tick next to those notes which you think are useful and clear.

There were probably as many reasons for coming to America as there were people who came. It was a highly individual decision. Yet it can be said that three large forces — religious persecution, political oppression and economic hardship — provided the chief motives for the mass migrations to our shores. They were responding, in their own way, to the pledge of the Declaration of Independence: the promise of 'life, liberty and the pursuit of happiness.'

The search for freedom of worship has brought people to America from the days of the Pilgrims to modern times. In our own day, for example, anti-Semitic and anti-Christian persecution in Hitler's Germany and the Communist empire have driven people from their homes to seek refuge in America. Not all found what they sought immediately. The Puritans of the Massachusetts Bay Colony, who drove Roger Williams and Anne Hutchinson into the wilderness, showed as little tolerance for dissenting beliefs as the Anglicans of England had shown to them. Minority religious sects, from the Quakers and Shakers through the Catholics and Jews to the Mormons and Jehovah's Witnesses, have at various times suffered both discrimination and hostility in the United States.

But the very diversity of religious belief has made for religious toleration. In demanding freedom for itself, each sect had increasingly to permit freedom for others. The insistence of each successive wave of immigrants upon its right to practice its religion helped make freedom of worship a central part of the American creed. People who gambled their lives on the right to believe in their own God would not lightly surrender that right in a new society.

The second great force behind immigration has been political oppression. America has always been a refuge from tyranny. As a nation conceived in liberty, it has held out to the world the promise of respect for the rights of man. Every time a revolution has failed in Europe, every time a nation has succumbed to tyranny, men and women who love freedom have assembled their families and their belongings and set sail across the seas. Nor has this process come to an end in our own day. The Russian Revolution, the terrors of Hitler's Germany and Mussolini's Italy, the Communist suppression of the Hungarian Revolution of 1956, and the cruel measures of the Castro regime in Cuba — all have brought new thousands seeking sanctuary in the United States.

The economic factor has been more complex than the religious and political factors. From the very beginning, some have come to America in

hardship difficulties

shores country

pledge promise

dissenting beliefs religious groups different from the Puritans.

creed belief

gambled risked

surrender give up

cheap labor workers who are paid a low salary

supply the number of people who emigrated to the USA.

A

Reasons for coming to America:
- belief in the Declaration of Independence
- search for freedom of worship (e.g. the Puritans of the Massachusetts Bay Colony who persecuted Roger Williams + Anne Hutchinson; persecution of the Quakers, Shakers, Catholics, Jews, Mormons ...)
- political oppression
- Revolutions + tyranny in Europe.
- economic factors (looking for riches, flying from poverty, no choice.)
- industrialization in America.

B

Many reasons for coming to America:
1. Religious persecution
   - no religious freedom found at the beginning.
   - but tolerance now.
2. Political oppression
   - e.g. in Europe
   - e.g. in the whole world
3. Economic hardship
   - searching for riches
   - flying from poverty
   - forced to go there
4. Need for cheap labor in the USA.

search of riches, some in flight from poverty and some because they were bought and sold and had no choice.

The process of industrialization in America increased the demand for cheap labor, and chaotic economic conditions in Europe increased the supply.

C

Many reasons for coming to America, but mainly 3:
I. Religious persecution
   eg. persecution against Jews in Hitler's Germany.
   a/ At first, many examples of intolerance and persecution in the USA.
   e.g. hostility against the Quakers + Shakers
   b/ But the USA has now become a tolerant country.
II. Political oppression
   America has always been a refuge from tyranny.
   e.g. Russian Revolution
        Castro regime in Cuba.
III. Economic hardship.
   a/ 3 main types
      • search for riches
      • flying from poverty
      • slavery
   b/ Immigration encouraged in the USA
   industrialization → demand for cheap labor.

D

Several reasons can explain why so many immigrants came to America. A first reason was the search for freedom of worship. Although the immigrants did not always find tolerance at once (for ex. the Puritans of Massachussetts did not accept any religion other than their own). America soon permitted religious freedom for everybody. Political oppression also drove a lot of people to America, people who were trying to flee from tyranny at home. A third reason must be mentioned — the economic one: the immigrants wanted to become rich and labor was wanted in America.

A ☐   B ☐   C ☐   D ☐

Why did you reject the other notes? (More than one answer is possible.)

Reasons for rejecting notes	Notes you rejected for this reason
1 not notes, but a summary	
2 mention of unimportant details	
3 important information not mentioned	
4 wrong structure	
5 wrong information	
6 the structure does not appear clearly	

Task 2

As with some of the other writing styles studied in this book, when
we take notes we omit certain words, and other items, for the sake
of speed. Tick any of the following which have been omitted from the
set of notes which you chose in Task 1.

- [ ] *There is/are* at the beginning of a sentence
- [ ] full verbs
- [ ] verb *to be*
- [ ] auxiliary verb *to have*
- [ ] prepositions
- [ ] *and*
- [ ] direct and indirect articles
- [ ] full stops

Task 3

In pairs, read through and study the following passage on food.

THE FOOD WE EAT

What your body needs

The energy value of food is measured in calories — units of heat. A man
lying in bed all day would need about 1700 calories a day to prevent him
from losing weight. If he got up and did an hour or so of light work, like
typing, he would need about another 75 calories. An hour's walking would
add another 150 and an hour's hard work, like digging the garden, would
mean another 300 or so. Needs vary with the weight of the body, but on
the whole the amount of food needed depends on the work done.

Modern nutritional science has made it possible, therefore, to design
standard diets for miners, office-workers, housewives and schoolchildren.
This means, for example, that in war-time food can be shared out fairly
and efficiently. In peace-time it enables people to judge their food
requirements accurately in the interests of their health.

No less important than the quantity of food we eat is its quality.
Everyone needs an adequate and balanced diet to help them keep warm
and fight off disease, and children in particular need good food to allow
them to grow up strong and healthy. There are three main categories of
foodstuffs and a good diet comprises balanced amounts of all three. One
of the most basic types of foods is carbohydrates, like starch (the main
constituent of grain) and sugar. In practice, whether most people have
enough to eat or not depends on whether they have enough
carbohydrates to fill them up — usually in the form of wheat, rice or
potatoes. The second main type of foodstuff is protein, like meat, fish,
cheese, eggs and milk. These are less important as a source of energy
and heat but vital for building up bones, teeth and body tissue. Adequate
protein is, therefore, particularly important for infants and growing
children and milk is a very good source of protein. The third type of food,

fats, provide concentrated energy. In Britain the most popular source of fats is butter.

The body also has a number of special needs for small quantities of substances like calcium phosphate, for bones and teeth (calcium and phosphorus are found in milk and cheese), and a number of minerals, like iron, iodine and sodium chloride (common salt). In addition to these the body requires an adequate intake of vitamins, substances essential to life, which are derived from certain specific foods.

Our Daily Bread Richard Tames

Now decide whether the statements in the table below are the main ideas of the text. If not, they may be secondary or supporting ideas, examples or digressions.

	Main idea	*Secondary idea, example, digression*
1 With an hour's walk, you need an extra 150 calories.		
2 Your need in calories varies with the amount of work you do.		
3 During a war, food can be shared in a fair way.		
4 A good diet should be balanced.		
5 Starch is the main constituent of grain.		
6 Proteins are not really a source of energy and heat.		
7 Butter is the most popular source of fats in Britain.		
8 Iron is essential for the body.		
9 Vitamins are essential to life.		

Task 4

Complete the list below to show the main ideas of the text. As you do so, write down all the link words which introduce each new idea.

Main ideas	Link words
1	
a *amount of food needed depends on type of work done . . .*	
b	*therefore*
. . . .	
2	
a 3 main categories of foodstuffs	
1 *carbohydrates (starch & sugar)*	
2	*The second*
3	
b other substances required	
1	
. . . .	
2	

3 Consolidation

In order to pick out the main points of a passage, to make notes, there are certain textual clues to the structure of the text to look out for.

Usually a new *paragraph* contains a new idea, while *link-words and phrases* show the structure of the text.

Task 1

In pairs, read the groups of link words and phrases on the next page. Match them with the functions that follow them.

link words and phrases

a So we can say that
In other words
To conclude

b first
then

firstly
secondly
thirdly

one point
another point
a last point

finally

c at that time
in 1962

before
previously
formerly

then
afterwards
next

while
as
during
meanwhile

d but
however
nevertheless
yet
in spite of what we said
although we said that
on the other hand
all the same
the trouble is that

e indeed
in other words
truly
that is to say

f because/since
the reason why

consequently
so
therefore
as a result
thus
then

g for example
for instance
an example of
this is clearly seen in
thus

h moreover
what's more

functions

☐ to express a time-relationship
☐ to list a number of points or ideas
☐ to express a cause or a consequence
☐ to express an idea which is contrary to what has been said before
☐ to introduce examples or illustrations
☐ to rephrase what has been said, or underline it
☐ to sum up what has been said
☐ to introduce another argument supporting an idea already mentioned

Task 2

Read the following passage and underline all the words and phrases used to signal the different ideas of the text. Some examples have been done for you.

<u>Quite apart from</u> the economic similarity between present-day automation and the mechanization which has been proceeding for centuries, <u>it must also be stressed that even</u> in the United States automation is by no means the only factor displacing people from existing jobs.

The increasing number of unneeded workers in recent years <u>has been the result of</u> much more simple and old-fashioned influences: farm labourers have been put out of work by bigger tractors, miners by the cheapness of oil, and railwaymen by better roads.

It is quite wrong, therefore, to think of automation as some new monster whose arrival threatens the existence of employment in the same way that the arrival of myxomatosis threatened the existence of the rabbit. Automation is one aspect of technological change, which itself is only one of the several changes (changes in tastes, changes in social patterns, changes in organization) which result in certain jobs disappearing and certain skills ceasing to be required. And even in America, which has a level of technology and output per head much in advance of Britain's, there is no evidence that the pace of change is actually speeding up.

Nevertheless changes in the amount of labour needed to produce a certain output are proceeding fairly rapidly in America — and in other countries — and may proceed more rapidly in future. Indeed it is one of the main objects of economic policy.

4 Extension

It is a waste of time to try to take down every word of a lecture. When making notes on a lecture or text, you will find this set of abbreviations and symbols useful.

cf.	refer (to)	+	plus/more
e.g.	for example	—	minus/less
etc.	et cetera/and so on	>	greater than/superior to
ibid.	in the same book or passage	<	less than/inferior to
i.e.	that is	→	from … to …/leads to …/results in
NB	note well (something important)	&	and
=/≠	is equal to/not the same as	∴	therefore
≃	about/around	∵	because

Task 1

The following notes were made on the entry about the Island of
Mauritius in the *Encyclopaedia Britannica.* No abbreviations have
been used, so that the notes are longer than necessary. Rewrite the
notes using abbreviations when possible.

MAURITIUS ISLAND

Mauritius, an island and independent member of the Commonwealth of
Nations in the Indian Ocean, lies about 500 miles East of the Malagasy
Republic.
The island is pear-shaped, about 38 miles long and 29 miles wide, with an
area of 720 square miles.

Physical geography:
Mauritius is wholly volcanic but contrary to Réunion, its neighbour, the
whole coastline is surrounded by a coral reef.
The highest summit is in the Southwest of the island but there are a
certain number of peaks almost as high, such as the Pieter Both.

Climate:
From April to October, the climate is mild, even chilly on the high ground.
From November to March the weather is hot and humid and during this
part of the year the island is sometimes visited by cyclones. Rainfall is
heavier in the central uplands (200 ins.) than on the West Coast, near
Port Louis (40 ins.).

The economy:
The island is almost entirely dependent on the cultivation of sugar-cane;
it occupies two-fifths of the whole island and more than four-fifths of the
arable land.
Some tea has been grown for many years on the central uplands
mentioned above, because of the rainfall.
The sugar and tea factories are the largest industrial enterprises, but it is
to be noted that a vigorous program for the encouragement of new
industries led to the establishment of a large number of new light
industrial plants.

The people:
The population increases (according to the 1982 census) at a rate of
about 3% a year, which causes alarm, and now reaches 963,900
inhabitants.
The main ethnic community, that is the Indian community, represents
69.5% of the population. Next come the Creole (28%) and Chinese (2.4%)
communities.
There are also Europeans, such as French, English, and others.

Politics and economy:
World recession, the effects of three cyclones and record unemployment
all contributed to the victory of the socialist Mauritius Militant Movement.

Task 2

Now take notes from the following text.

THE AMERICAN FAMILY AFTER WORLD WAR II

Changing social attitudes. To the surprise of observers who had expected a continuation of prewar familiar trends (Chapter 23), the American family showed remarkable stability during the postwar decades. The divorce rate was high, to be sure (about one in four marriages failed), but so was the marriage rate; and the old tradition of the large family came surging back, after an understandable decline during the lean depression years.

Moreover, children more than ever became the center of attention in most families. Parents who themselves had known hardship and want as children in the thirties, now overcompensated by shielding their own young from life's difficulties. In middle-class homes, the tendency was to indulge children their every whim and to plan the family's every activity in terms of whatever was 'good for the kids.' As historian John Brooks commented, 'Children seem to be born believing that they enjoy full equal rights with their parents, and our society encourages — very nearly compels — them to retain that belief.'

Children also grew up learning more about 'life' from television than from reading books or talking with parents. Together with parental permissiveness, indeed, television helped to shape the social attitudes of the postwar young in ways profoundly significant for the future. On the one hand, in the wholly passive process of 'receiving' whatever television offered them, many young people failed to develop a capacity for rational discourse or critical analysis. On the other hand, the medium's emphasis on action, often purely for its own sake, taught many young viewers the false notion that 'instant gratification' of one's needs and desires was the normal condition of life.

For American women, the postwar decades did little to resolve the dilemma posed by the seeming conflict between motherhood and career. In the 1950s, the tendency was toward a revival of domesticity. Among middle-class women, the concern for social activism of the war and prewar years gave way to a conviction that motherhood was a woman's highest duty and most fulfilling role. Television, women's magazines, and the retail sales industry exploited this 'feminine mystique.' In a book of that title in 1964, Betty Friedan argued strongly that woman's place was not in the home, but rather in a career.

In fact, even as the marriage and birth rates soared, more and more women went to work. By 1960, they made up a third of the total labor force and held an impressively large share of the national wealth. Yet, as a group they were among the exploited workers in the economy. Paid less than men for comparable work and usually discriminated against in promotions, they were also confined largely to certain kinds of work, even when they were fully qualified by education for other duties.

In the general re-awakening of social consciousness in the 1960s, a 'women's liberation movement' emerged, demanding full equality of women with men. Unfortunately, the leaders of 'women's lib' differed sharply among themselves as to precise goals. Perhaps in its very nature, the dilemma of home versus career was an unresolvable one.

The Shaping of America, R. Curry, J. Sproat & K. Cramer

When you have completed your notes, give them to your partner. Each of you then writes up a new passage from the notes. When you have completed that, compare the two new versions with each other and the original. Have you included all the main points?

The activities and exercises in this unit are designed to practise several of the types of written English you have studied in this book.

Task 1 Who wrote it?

Look at the picture below, choose one character, and write a short text he or she could have written. You can choose anything — a telegram, a postcard, a diary — which could have been written a short time before or after this picture was taken. There are two examples to give you some ideas.

Putting it all together

Example texts:	type	written by	to whom?	when?	why?
Dear Bill Wonderful weather and met a great girl, but running out of cash. Need a windfall or I'll soon be home again looking for work. Yours, Sam	postcard	the thief	friend	before	asking for help? or just a friendly postcard?
SEND MONEY AT ONCE STOP LETTER FOLLOWS LOVE TOM	Telegram	the man in the deck-chair	friends	after	his wallet was stolen

When you have written your own text, work in pairs. Show your text to your partner and ask him or her to find out:

- which of the characters wrote it
- to whom it was written
- when and why it was written

Then try the same exercise with other pictures of your choice.

Task 2 Fit the phrase

This activity can be done either in pairs or in groups of up to four. Consider the following phrase: *the complete works of Shakespeare* and think where it could have been written (e.g. in a message; a postcard; a letter; a diary). Write out the whole text (not too long). Then compare your results with your partner's, or with other people's in your group. You may be surprised to see how many different interpretations one phrase can take on when put in context.

Example

```
                                        20 Market Street,
                                        Haltwhistle,
                                        Northumberland,
                                        NE49 0DX

                                        14th April 1987
The Manager,
Classic Books,

4 Grey Street,
Newcastle-upon-Tyne
NE1 8ST


Dear Sir or Madam,

I would be grateful if you would send me one hardback copy of the
Complete Works of Shakespeare.  Please charge it to my account.

Yours faithfully,

Gregory Smith

GREGORY SMITH
```

Here are some more phrases.

a cherry tree
marmalade cat
pink limousine
Foreign Minister

Now, in your pairs or groups, each person thinks of a phrase for the same treatment. (Each person thinks of a context for each phrase.)

Task 3 Job applications

Look through the following job advertisements. This time, the applications are to be made over the telephone. To make sure you give the right information clearly and quickly, note down what you want to say, and in what order. The first one has been done for you.

M. GOFF
PAINTERS, DECORATORS
REQUIRED

Long term work prospects. Good rates and conditions. All areas London and Home Counties.

Apply: Michael Goff Coatings Limited
Finlay House, 140 High Street, Berkhamsted, Herts
Tel: 04427 71984

ACCOUNTS CLERK/
VDU OPERATOR
£6,500 p.a. max

Busy office 10 minutes Hammersmith Broadway. Must have at least 3 years relevant experience in accounts office. Monday to Friday, 9 am-5 pm, four weeks holiday.

Phone Mrs. Martell on 01-741 1231 ext. 224.

A MIDDLESEX COUNTY PRESS NEWSPAPER

Earn Extra Money

by delivering the Leader newspaper to homes in this area — and you get paid in cash every week!

So if you're over 13 years of age call us on **Uxbridge (0895) 37161 Extension 419 between 9 a.m. and 5 p.m. Monday-Friday.** (We will need to know your postcode).

YOUNG REPORTER/FEATURE WRITER

needed by expanding West London agency producing house journals with national circulations.

He/she will work with experienced industrial editors and under the direction of a former Fleet Street chief sub.

Good mix of stories to cover, some travel in UK. Starting salary £8,000 p.a. plus bonus.

Applications and CVs to Brian Cummings & Partners, Lamerton House, 23a High Street, London W5 5DF. Tel. 01-579 9190.

TYRE FITTERS

Tyreservices Great Britain require Commercial Tyrefitters and Car Tyrefitters for their branch in Battersea. Good rate of pay and bonus. For early interview please telephone Branch Manager on

01-223 1248

Vandenwal Motor Ltd need to fill the following vacancies:-

FULLY SKILLED
MOTOR MECHANICS

Applicants should be fully conversant with Ford Motor Vehicles. Top basic wage. 37½ hour week plus time saved bonus.

PART-TIME
MAINTENANCE PERSON

Would suit retired builder. To look after the maintenance of our garage. Must be able to work on own initiative. Pay and hours to be agreed.

To apply to either of these vacancies please call Mr. D. Grant on:-

01-870 8980

Handwritten notes:

1. 223 1248 – Branch Manager
2. have been working as tyre fitter in Hammersmith ABC Tyres.
3. Saw ad in Hammersmith and Fulham Guardian.
4. Moving to Wandsworth
5. Can supply references
6. Available for interview any time

Now exchange your notes with a partner. Write your partner's notes up as a formal letter of application.

Task 4 Write it for them!

Choose a well-known character (contemporary or historical, real or fictional) and write something he or she could have written. It can be in any of the forms of written English you have studied in this book — even if that would be historically incorrect (e.g. a telegram before they were invented!).

A variation of this exercise would be to omit the name of the writer, and give the text to your partner for him/her to guess who wrote it.

A further variation would be to work in groups of four. Each person writes the name of a character on a piece of paper, and a type of writing (taken from those in this book) on another.

For example:

Fold and mix the papers, keeping them in two separate piles (i.e. person and writing type). Each member of the group takes a piece of paper from each pile and writes what is demanded. You each read them out to the rest of your group once you have all finished.

Key

UNIT 1

1 Familiarization

Task 1

The only unlikely occasion is of a business letter.

Task 2

1 Greeting
  B *Dear Mr Thompson,*
  C *Dear Aunt Elizabeth,*
  D *My dear Anne,*

2 Salutation
  A *Best wishes,*
  B *Sincerely yours,*
  C *Love,*
  D *Lots of love, Love & kisses,*

3 Contractions
  A *hotel's we're don't*
  B *we'll*
  C *I've, we'll, I'll, you're*
  D *don't, can't*

4 Omissions
  B (I am) *looking forward* . . .
  C (I) *am thinking* . . . (I) *hope* . . .
  D (We) *are on our way* . . .
    (We) *have little time to* . . .
    (We) *hope the weather* . . .

5 Type of omissions
  personal pronouns (*I, we*)

Task 3

Postcard A: possibly a colleague with whom the writer is
          friendly — *Don't work too hard* . . .
Postcard B: acquaintance — *Yours,*
          Dennis Parsons (surname a bit formal)
Postcard C: nephew to aunt — *Dear Aunt Elizabeth,*
Postcard D: a close friend — greeting, salutation, *We*
          miss you

Task 4

1 A What a lovely place Switzerland is, especially under
    the snow! The hotel's perfect, the food delicious —
  B Dartmoor is really picturesque or rather what I can
    see of it in the pouring rain!
  C Jaipur is a hot and humid place to work in . . .

2 A Even the dog enjoys playing in the snow and we have
    all greatly improved our skiing style.
  B We are walking about 20 miles every day and so far
    have visited Exeter and Okehampton.
  C . . . I am thoroughly enjoying the conference on
    tropical diseases. We sometimes work late at night.

  D Are on our way to Tours but have little time to write
    because we lost all our luggage and papers and Joe is
    being held up at the police station.
    . . . we all have colds and can't get the tent to dry.

3 A Tomorrow we're going skating on the lake.
  B We really want to try and reach Plymouth, then we'll
    start thinking about coming home.
  C . . . but we'll soon get a few days off. Am thinking of
    going shopping in Bombay. I'll bring you back a sari
    and plenty of tea!

4 A Don't work too hard and take care of yourself.
  B Looking forward to seeing you soon.
  C Hope you're feeling better after your operation.
  D The trip was so boring without you.
    We miss you.

2 Transfer and practice

Task 1

2 Next week we'll probably be back home with you.
3 Yesterday we drove along the Loire Valley.
4 Today we're enjoying the sun and doing nothing.
5 Everyday we go for a walk.
6 Last week we spent 2 days in Corfu.
7 Lately (recently) it's been extremely cold.
8 So far we've had rain every day.
a 3, 6 **b** 1, 2 **c** 4 **d** 7, 8 **e** 5

Task 2

Sentences you could write at the end of the second day
are:
1, 3, 4, 5, 6, 7, 8.

3 Consolidation

Task 2
(suggested answer)

Dear Jane,
  Having a wonderful time back in Devon again.
  Spent Monday riding on Dartmoor with Matthew who fell
off 3 times! Was he cross!
  Weather OK so have been swimming though beaches are
horribly crowded.
  Went to Exeter last night for a beautiful but huge meal.
  See you soon,
  Lots of love,
    Angie

UNIT 2

1   Familiarization

Task 1

1 a school boy (maths homework)
NB The Samaritans are an organization who have people manning the telephone 24 hours a day for those in despair to ring them.
2 an army officer during a war
3 an explorer? traveller in Africa probably or Asia?
4 a parent — C probably the son

The extracts are from published diaries — real or fictional.
1 *The Secret Diary of Adrian Mole Aged 13¾*. Sue Townsend.
2 *D Day*. J. Gunther
3 *Black Mischief*. Evelyn Waugh.
4 *Edith's Diary*. Patricia Highsmith.

Task 3

1 Day of the week and date usually given.
  1 Monday January 25th
  2 Sunday July 25
  3 March 14th, Monday
2 a Diary 1 (*couldn't do . . ./phoned*)
    Diary 3 (*Met caravan*)
    Diary 4 (*Did not find it. Have no doubt*)
  b Diary 3 *Hideous night* (*I/We spent a . . .*)
              Up and dressed (*Got up and got dressed*)
  c Diary 3 *No news [of] Sarah's trunk*
3 a Diary 4 *C.*
  b *v.* (very) *etc.* (etcetera)

2   Transfer and practice

Task 1

1 in 2 at (after) 3 for 4 after 5 since
6 for (during) 7 during 8 at (about)

Task 2

(Suggested diary entry)
Today fine at first but went wrong later on. Guests arrived in good time for drinks. Had lunch by pool. Afterwards relaxed and talked. Soon it got hot so most guests decided to have a swim in the pool. Then an extraordinary thing happened — by some amazing accident a whirlpool started sucking in swimmers. Soon there were shouts, screams, panic. Finally F switched the filter off and at last all was OK. But all were *v.* frightened, no one really hurt. We of course horribly embarrassed.

3   Consolidation

Task 1

Home at last after a long sleepless night. Something incredible happened yesterday.
Had just got to the station *after* a hard day's work. Was just about to board the train *when* suddenly all the lights went out. *At first there was* a real panic *especially during* the first five minutes, people screamed and rushed to the street thinking it was the end of the world. *Soon, however*

they started to calm down and patiently waited for the electricity to come back. But I *quickly* realized it was useless to wait there. So *took to* the streets, but everything dark there. Didn't know what to do, where to go.
Tried to stay in town but all hotels full.
Spent the night on a bench in Central Park — not very comfortable! Could not even go to sleep!
Managed to get a lift home at *around* 5 a.m. Was dropped 3 miles away from here. So *had to walk!*
Am *finally* home *but* absolutely exhausted. *Shall have* a bath and go to bed.

Task 4

From *The Diary of a Tulip* by Keith Waterhouse (*Pick of Punch*, 1981).

UNIT 3

1   Familiarization

Task 1

All are possible occasions for sending messages.

Task 2

The order in which the messages were written is:
B C A D
Mr and Mrs Dennis were expected at Pete's house for dinner but they couldn't get their car out of the garage as someone else's car had broken down and was blocking the entrance. They rang Pete to say that they would be late and to start dinner without them. Somebody took their message. When they arrived Pete had already left. The dinner was burnt and he'd gone to a pizzeria. He didn't say *which* one he'd gone to so his friends couldn't join him. They left him the ice-cream that they'd brought for supper on the door step!

Task 3

Type of word		Examples
√	(to) be	A *Dinner (is) burnt!*
		B *(I'm) sorry I'm blocking your garage.*
√	(to) have	A *(Have) gone to pizzeria . . .*
×	other verbs	
×	nouns	
√	pronouns	A *(I/We) 've gone to pizzeria . . .*
		B *(I)'m sorry I'm . . .*
		(I) can't release . . .
		(I) will get mechanic
		C *(They) can't use their car.*
		(They) said not to wait for them.
		D *. . . to enjoy ice-cream we brought (you)!*
√	articles	A *(The) dinner*
		B *(the) handbrake*
		(a) mechanic
		(the) pizzeria
		D *(the) ice-cream*

2   Transfer and practice

Task 1

Explaining what happened

A Dinner burnt. Gone to pizzeria . . . .

B can't use their car.

D Can't release handbrake.

Apologizing

D Sorry I'm blocking your garage.

Explaining plans

B Mr & Mrs Dennis will be late.

D Will get mechanic tommorrow.

Wishes

C Hope you come back in time to enjoy ice-cream we brought!

Giving instructions

A Come and join us.

B said not to wait for them.

Task 2

(suggested answer)

Had to go to the hospital to see mother. No time to cook your supper.

Went to bed at 2 a.m. Your supper still in oven! Suggest you sleep on sofa.

Tell Jim and Fred | to lock | the front door.
               | not to bang |

UNIT 4

1   Familiarization

Task 1

The unlikely ones are to apply for a job, to complain and to order goods by post.

2   Letters of invitation

Task 1

We would be very happy if you and Simon could join us. Do come if you can.

Task 2

(suggested answer)

Dear Claire,

   Thank you so much for your nice long letter. I meant to *write ages ago* but somehow I *never have time these days*.

   The thing is we are having *a supper party* next *Wednesday 28th July, to celebrate* our tenth wedding anniversary with *a few old friends*. It will be quite informal as Paul hates dressing up. We *would be delighted* if *you could join us. Can you be here* at 8 p.m.

   We *look forward to seeing you.*

   Love,

   Jane

3   Letters of acceptance or refusal

Task 1

See Key for Guide to letter writing at end of this unit.

Task 2

Relationship	Acceptance/ Refusal	What	Expressions
1 wife to husband	acceptance	meet her husband at airport	*Of course the answer will have to be yes.*
2 a friend — he is fond of her but doesn't see her often	refusal	party invitation	*I'm afraid I won't be able to make it to your party.*
3 teacher/tutor to ex-student	acceptance	addressee wants to come and stay	*I (. . .) will be only too delighted for you to come and stay for a couple of nights.*

Task 3

Phrases you could use to express acceptance

I | should | be delighted to . . .
  | would |

Of course, we'll . . .

We'll come with pleasure . . .

Thank you so much for your invitation. We're looking forward to seeing you . . .

Yes, we'll be there . . .

Phrases you could use to express refusal

I would love to come, but . . .

It would have been lovely to join you, but . . .

It was nice of you to suggest it, but . . .

I wish I could accept your kind invitation . . .

I'm afraid we won't be able to join you all . . .

Unfortunately we will not be able to . . .

Phrases you could use to express either (depending on what follows them)

What a surprise to get your invitation . . .

It's such a long time since we last met so . . .

Task 4

Wednesday Nov. 20th

Dear Frances,

   Thank you for inviting me over next weekend. It would have been lovely to see you both. Unfortunately I don't think I'll be able to come. I'm busy all day Saturday and on Sunday afternoon. I could cancel my tennis on Sunday morning but that wouldn't leave me more than a couple of hours to spend with you.

   Perhaps I could organize something at my house in the near future. Thanks again for the invitation.

With love,

Alison

4   Letters of thanks

Task 1

1 c   2 b   3 e   4 d   5 a

Task 2

1 Thank you for your extremely generous Christmas present.
2 How very kind of you to remember me at Christmas!
3 I can't tell you how touched I am that you still go on remembering us . . .
4 I must admit I had been secretly hoping that someone would give me socks — and you did!
5 I must write at once to thank you for your magnificent present.

5   Letters of apology

Task 1

Any are possible — a letter to a boss might well be formal, as could some of the others, depending on the circumstances.

Task 2

Dear Peter,
I'm sorry about last night. I didn't mean to spoil your party, but your boss was very irritating. *Please excuse me* for what I said. You know how worked up I get when people talk politics; I lose all my self-control. So when he started going on about this new political scandal, I just couldn't keep my mouth shut. I should have kept out of it all. *Sorry*, Peter! I just hope you will get your promotion all right. It was all my fault, I was your guest; next time I'll behave myself, I promise!
Best wishes,
Paul

Dear Mr Miller,
I am awfully sorry for what happened yesterday. I'm afraid I must have spoiled your party and I feel really bad about it all. *I do apologize* for my disgraceful behaviour. I should never have started talking about politics. When your boss mentioned this new political scandal, I knew I would lose my temper; I should have kept off the subject. *Do excuse me, please!* I hope this will not affect your promotion in any way. I know the party was very important to you and it was inexcusable of me to behave as I did.
Yours,
Paul Mason

Task 3

Phrases which express apology

 1 I'm very/terribly/extremely sorry
 2 I'd like to apologize for . . .
 5 please forgive me for . . .
 6 I really must apologize for . . .
10 sorry to have done this/for doing this
12 you must forgive me for . . .
14 please accept my apologies for . . .
15 how stupid of me!
17 you'll have to excuse me
 3 and **16** express concern or dismay.
4, 7, 8, 9, 11; 13 are expressions that might be used to

accept an apology.

Guide to letter writing (page 30)

3 My darling, My dear Julia, Dear Uncle Arthur,
4 Thank you so much for your nice long letter,
  I was awfully glad to get your card,
  I meant to write before.
5 I am awfully sorry for what happened yesterday; Thank you for your awfully generous Christmas present; Come and have a meal with us; Of course the answer will have to be yes; I'm afraid I won't be able to make it to your party;
6 We look forward to seeing you.
  Perhaps I could organize something at my house in the near future.
7   I love you so much,
    Lots of love,/much love,
    Love,
    Best wishes,/All the best,
    Yours,
    Yours sincerely,
    Yours truly,

UNIT 5

1   Familiarization

Task 2

1 d, a, g, f.
2 e, j, h, b, i, c.

Task 3

(suggested answer)

1 Ross left his dog with Charles. The dog was unbearable so Charles wanted it collected. Ross told Charles to take the dog back home, but it had to go to the RSPCA (Royal Society for the Prevention of Cruelty to Animals, a charity concerned with animal welfare). Neighbours were threatening court action. Ross sent details of his solicitor, and said he'd be back the next day.
2 Helena is staying longer in France, and asks Derek to change her London to Exeter ticket. He says he cannot, and she should buy another in London. But Helena has run out of money and wants Derek to send her £50. He says this is impossible. (A postal order is a way of sending money within the UK if you do not want to send cash or a cheque. They can be bought, for a fee plus the required sum, in Post Offices.) He suggested she ask Jane, obviously another friend, to help. So Helena asks for Jane's address, which Derek sends.

Task 4

(suggested answers)

1 **d** Your dog is unbearable! Please come and get it immediately!
  a Please take the dog round to my house. I'll be back in three days.
  g Your neighbours have been disturbed by the dog's barking and have taken out a court action against you. The dog has been removed by the RSPCA.

f Can you contact my solicitor, Mr Jones? I will be back tomorrow.

2 e I've been delayed and shan't return till Sunday. Please change my London to Exeter train ticket for me in England. (This suggests she can't change it in France.)

j It's impossible to do that here. You'll have to buy another one in London.

h I haven't got any money left. Please send me £50.

b It's impossible to send postal orders to France. Ask Jane to help you.

i Please send me Jane's address.

c Jane's address is Jane Turner, 4, Townsend Street, London. (Note that without at least a district number — e.g. SW11 — or preferably a full post code, this address is not really sufficient, and the letter might not reach Jane.)

Two other points to notice: use of capital letters (for clarity when you complete the form, and as printed when you receive it); no punctuation other than STOP to end a sentence.

2 Practice and consolidation

Task 1

(suggested answer)

(TO) (name)

(ADDRESS AND TELEPHONE NO) 10 ROOSEVELT AVE

(CITY — STATE & ZIP CODE) HERTFORD MD 893241

BRIEFCASE STOLEN STOP SEND ADDRESS BOOK DESK DRAWER STOP ARRANGE DUPLICATE DRIVER'S LICENCE STOP TELL ANNA TO PHOTOCOPY CONFERENCE TALK AND SEND SPARE URGENTLY STOP SEND $200 STOP

(SENDER'S TEL NO) 741 29 43 (NAME & AD) (name)

RAMADA RENAISSANCE
SAN FRANCISCO

(38 words = $19)

Note — use your family name (surname) only to save words. The number and street count as one word. Zip code is US usage — postcode is UK usage.

Task 2

(suggested answer)

(TO) JAMES

30 DANE STREET

SOUTHAMPTON

S09 4YQ

CLAPHAM LONDON SW12

SLIGHT ACCIDENT STOP ALL WELL BUT NEED REST AND CAR REPAIRS STOP SEND £300 STOP RING INSURANCE TO CONFIRM ALL OK DETAILS IN DESK DRAWER STOP TELL JANE TUESDAY OFF STOP SONIA

INVERNESS 3478   WALTER SCOTT INN
INVERNESS

(38 words = £9.50)

UNIT 6

1 Familiarization

Task 1

You would be most likely to write formal letters to apply for a job, complain about faulty goods and in correspondence with your bank manager.

2 Letters of application

Task 1

J. Hoop is unlikely to get the job as it is badly constructed and badly spelled.

Prospective employers like to receive letters which are correctly spelled, and which detail your qualifications and relevant experience. They should be short and to the point.

NB This is a 'joke' letter from a British magazine called *Punch* which contains humorous articles and cartoons.

Task 4

(possible answers)

Dear Sirs,

   With reference to your advertisement in yesterday's *Pullman's Gazette* for the post of personal secretary, I should like to apply for the post.

   I feel that my qualifications match your requirements. I enclose my curriculum vitae. . . . the names and addresses of two referees.

   I am available for interview at any time which would suit you.

   Yours faithfully,
   (signature)
   EVA MARSHALL (MS)

3 Letters of complaint

Task 1

You might write a formal letter of complaint when you have been sold poor quality goods, when a train was late, when you didn't receive something you ordered by post and when you had a bad meal in a restaurant.

You might complain when something was stolen if you were somewhere where you felt there should have been sufficient security — e.g. if you were in a hotel and your valuables were kept in the hotel safe.

As for your neighbours — you would be more likely to speak to them, or possibly write an informal note.

Task 2

Dear Sir or Madam,

   I saw your advertisement for '*the perfect lighter*' in the Sunday Times last week and immediately sent *off a £2 postal order and the completed form* in order to *receive the lighter*.

   Imagine my surprise when all I got in return was *a box of matches*! I could understand a mistake, I might even pardon a joke, but in this case, your advertisement is a deliberate lie since a friend of mine who also sent the coupon got the same result.

I think it's a shame to promise an economical lighter when in fact *you are not selling a lighter at all.* Instead of saying it works quickly, you should *admit that you are offering matches.* And what about 'only' £2: *I usually pay 10p for a box of matches, and they are often given away free.*

I regard your advertisement as a serious deception and demand that you send me *my money back* immediately. Otherwise I will take active steps to make sure the Consumers' Association hears about it.

Yours faithfully,

Task 3
likely order 3 2 1

Expressions of complaint:
Imagine my surprise when all I got in return was a box of matches!
. . . your advertisement is a deliberate lie.
I think it's a shame to promise an economical lighter . . .

Task 5
Components of a letter of complaint
a b e f g h i
Order of inclusion
a i b h f g/e

UNIT 7

1   Familiarization
Task 1
Any of these are possible. Obviously most letters won't be planned, but an important business letter or job application often will be. Even writing to a friend, one might jot down notes so as not to forget points.

Task 2
a can't tell; **b** can't tell? married? unlikely.
c presumably William IV's (and therefore George IV's?)
d can't tell **e** Liberal, probably **f** can't tell

2   Transfer and practice
Task 1
C is the best set of notes. B is the second best

Reasons for rejecting notes	*notes you rejected for this reason*
1 not notes, but a summary	D
2 mention of unimportant details	A
3 important information not mentioned	A, B
4 wrong structure	A, D
5 wrong information	A, D
6 the structure does not appear clearly	A, D

Task 2
Items omitted from notes (using C as best example)

There is/are at the beginning of a sentence.
full verbs
(*and* reduced to &)
direct and indirect articles
full stops

Task 3
1 example
2 main idea
3 example
4 main idea
5 digression
6 secondary idea
7 digression
8 example
9 digression

Task 4

main ideas	*link words*
1 The energy value of food is measured in calories.	
a amount of food needed depends on work done	*but on the whole*
b nutritional science means standard diets can be designed for different groups	*therefore*
2 Quality of food as important as quantity	*No less important than*
a 3 main categories of foodstuffs	
1 carbohydrates (starch and sugar)	*One of the*
2 protein (meat, fish, dairy products)	*The second*
3 fats (esp. butter)	*The third*
b other substances required	*also . . . like*
1 calcium phosphate minerals	*and . . . like*
2 vitamins	*in addition*

3   Consolidation
Task 1
c to express a time-relationship
b to list a number of points or ideas
f to express a cause or a consequence
d to express an idea which is contrary to what has been said before
g to introduce examples or illustrations
e to rephrase what has been said, or underline it
a to sum up what has been said
h to introduce another argument supporting an idea already mentioned.

Task 2
Quite apart from the economic similarity between present-day automation and the mechanization which has been proceeding for centuries, *it must also be stressed that*

even in the United States automation is by no means the only factor displacing people from existing jobs.

The increasing number of unneeded workers in recent years *has been the result of* much more simple and old-fashioned influences: farm labourers have been put out of work by bigger tractors, miners by the cheapness of oil, and railwaymen by better roads.

It is quite wrong, *therefore*, to think of automation as some new monster whose arrival threatens the existence of employment *in the same way that* the arrival of myxomatosis threatened the existence of the rabbit. Automation *is one aspect of* technological change, *which* itself is only one of *the several changes* (changes in tastes, changes in social patterns, changes in organization) *which result in* certain jobs disappearing and certain skills ceasing to be required. *And even* in America, *which* has a level of technology and output per head much in advance of Britain's, there is no evidence that the pace of change is actually speeding up.

Nevertheless changes in the amount of labour needed to produce a certain output are proceeding fairly rapidly in America — *and* in other countries — *and* may proceed more rapidly in future. *Indeed* it is one of the main objects of economic policy.

4 Extension

Task 1
(possible format for notes)
Mauritius
ind. member Commonwealth of Nations
Position
Indian Ocean 500m E Malagasy Rep.
pear shape 38m × 29m
area = 720 sq m
Physical geog
volcanic, surrounded coral reef
Highest mt. – SW Island (others sim. ht, e.g. Pieter Both)
Climate
April → Oct. mild (chilly high ground)
Nov. → March hot & humid (sometimes cyclones)
Rain central uplands → W. coast nr. Port Louis,
i.e. 200 in. v. 40 in.
Economy
1 sugar cane – 2/5 whole island, 4/5 arable land
2 tea – central uplands ∵ rain
3 move to encourage new ind. → many light ind. plants
People
Pop. incr. (c.f. 1982 census) 3% p.a.
Total 963,900
Ethnic groups: Indian 69.5%
                  Creole 28%
                  Chinese 2.4%
                  + Europeans (e.g. French, English)
Politics & econ.
World recess. + 3 cyclones + rec. unemploy. → socialist victory
Mauritius Militant Movement